6/29/11

Bruce,

Thank you
for all you do
to bring the finance
to bring the finest Staff
to Front Start

All the best,

FINDING THE FORTUNE

Praise for *FINDING THE FORTUNE*

"Informative, inspirational and thought provoking. A must read."
- Robin Korom
Vice President of Commercial Lending
Consumers Credit Union

Jean's book *Finding the Fortune* and her seminars on methods she described in the book are very practical and simple to follow. I have utilized her methods in my business with great results. I track my follow-up on white boards, so it reminds me of the activity necessary to convert a prospect to a customer. It's very simple, but it takes a great amount of effort which, in the end, really pays off. Many thanks to Jean for helping me to persist, keep my eye on the ball and reap the benefits!"
- Christine Hammerlund, RN.
President
Assured Healthcare Staffing

"Jean is one of the most motivated people I have ever met. Even with her busy schedule she always has time to help others find their own path. Her new book, *Finding the Fortune* is a great tool for any business owner to find success. I am honored that Jean included my contributing piece to this project. Upon reading the book, I found that every single chapter had information that I needed to successfully "Follow up" to increase my business. This is one of those books that delivers that "ah-ha" moment that can really impact your business."
- Jim Mecir
Jim Mecir, LLC

"Today, the reality is, people are buying more and more through the internet. Click - Buy - Save has affected just about every industry out there. It's hard to compete with a computer that is programmed to follow up with a consumer over and over unless we as salespeople are equipped with the proper tools illustrated in Jean's book. Jean's Book has been a valuable resource for me to use with my sales team!"
- Kevin Schwartz
President
Wm Schwartz & Co. Insurance

"Your writing on building relationships resonated with me and helped me realize that I have not done enough proper follow-up. This will help me to improve this. I will definitely be recommending your books to others."

- Dan Mendelevitz
Business Coach / Professional Speaker

"Her book is both motivating and problem-solving. I often read a chapter for a few minutes, and it gives me a fresh perspective on how to attack my day's activities."

- Mark Cohen
Business Performance Advisor
Insperity

Jean MacDonald exemplifies and lives philanthropically on a daily basis. She connects with everyone and connects people to others in a way that benefits the people she surrounds. Her credibility as a successful business woman, her reputation, and her success comes from supporting and adding value to others.

- John Edgcomb
President
Cutting Edge Connect,Inc.

"This is a must-read for any business owner that wants to be successful."

- Glen Nielsen
author of the book *Unvarnished Truth*

"I love your book, now that I finally sat down to read it! It is the simple in life that works so well!! Thanks for your refreshing outlook and vibrant personality!"

- Andrea Torf
Brand Partner
Nerium International

"I truly enjoyed this book. It was an easy read, simple to follow and to understand. I loved the notes section, which enables the reader to write down their thoughts as soon as they had read the previous chapter. This enables you to see the changes you need to make in order for you to follow the process, which is very well defined in the book. It also is a great tool to look back over to keep yourself in check and to follow the plan in the book. Great for business owners!"

- Aishling Dalton - Kelly
President
Aishling Companion Home Care, Inc.

Finding the Fortune was such a great read! "I was truly inspired by the personal experiences that Jean shared and her invaluable lessons learned about the importance of "Following up." This book describes, in detail, how easy it to have great success in your life and your business if you just follow Jean's simple system."

- Janet Silge
Market Partner
MONAT Global

"However beautiful the strategy,
you should occasionally
look at the results."

~ Winston Churchill ~

FINDING THE FORTUNE

How to Strengthen Your Follow-Up Strategies and Close More Sales

Jean MacDonald

FINDING THE FORTUNE
How to Strengthen Your Follow-Up Strategies and Close More Sales

Published by:
ACE Publish
919-704-8036
Chapel Hill, NC
www.AcePublish.com

Address all inquiries to:
Jean MacDonald
Telephone: (413) 222-7250
Email: Jean@JeanConnects.com
www.FindingTheFortune.com
www.NetworkConnectSucceed.com

ISBN: 978-0-9883022-4-2

Library of Congress Cataloging-in-Publication Data has been applied for.

Editor: Christine Schaefer
Cover Designer: Aaron W. Risi / Yo Arty Productions / (410) 746-7845
Interior Book Layout: Leslie Lipps / Your Marketing Department / (847) 223-2692
Author Photo: Jeff Mateer / Studio West Photography / (847) 362-9060

Every attempt has been made to properly source all quotes.

Printed in the United States of America

Second Addition publication March 2017

To order additional copies of this book, contact your favorite bookseller or call Jean MacDonald's office at (413) 222-7250

If you are unable to order this book from your local bookseller, you may order through www.NetworkConnectSucceed.com or Jean@JeanConnects.com.

Dedication

For Derek, Aaron & Laura
You are the new crop of
"Hot Tomatoes!"
You mean the world to me. I always
look to you for joy and laughter.
You can always count on me.
Love, *M*

Definitions

Fortune: the success or failure of a person or enterprise over a period of time or in the course of a particular activity.

Follow-up: an action or thing that serves to increase the effectiveness of a previous one, as a second or subsequent letter, phone call, or visit.

If the fortune lies in the follow-up, are you willing to do the work?
~ Jean MacDonald ~

Contents

Contents

Introduction

Sales people are notorious for chasing (not catching) business. What would it be like if, every day, you were organized and could sit down to a clean desk, with your roadmap ready for the day, and your week all planned out? What if you had put those new contacts in your contact manager and made the calls that would lead to the next piece of business? Would you actually be chasing that next client? Here's a way to alleviate all the stress that comes with chasing business: Follow-up, follow-up, follow-up! And then, follow through!

Dr. Kerry Johnson, business author and peak performance coach, once posed this question: "Do we need more time? Or do we need to be more disciplined with the time we have?" Mary Kay Ash, entrepreneur and founder of the Mary Kay Cosmetics empire, put it this way: "Those people blessed with the most talent don't necessarily outperform everyone else. It's the people with follow-through who excel."

Both these quotes, at the heart of them, express the importance of focus and determination in achieving your dreams and realizing your visions. The wisdom they offer is especially timely right now, when so many entrepreneurs, salespeople, and business owners seem to be running harder than ever just to keep up. Building relationships, running day-to-day operations, staying on top of technology and social media - they all require those most valuable of assets: your time, your energy and your creativity.

Beyond the Quotes
In my career, I have found the single, most essential aspect of operating a successful business to have timely, effective follow-up. Unfortunately, it is often the first task to fall by the wayside in the rush to keep up with countless other distractions. We often make excuses for not following up. We use our families as an excuse (after school activities, events, celebrations) instead of realizing that we are doing it FOR our family. Some other

excuses are: I don't have time today, so I'll call tomorrow; I'm not in the mood; that person is on vacation; I don't know whether to call, text, or email. And nothing gets done. Then before you know it, it's the end of the month and you're running around like a squirrel collecting nuts to make your sales goals and finish projects in order to meet the deadline. Because of this, you often don't have time to prepare and plan for the next month.

Excuses Aside

In my first book *"Get Up, Get Dressed and Get Out the Door!"* I noted that if you are on this treadmill to nowhere, you need to STOP, regroup, and put things into perspective. The drama surrounding getting things started, starts with you. NO EXCUSES.

Here's the bottom line: a survey of nearly one thousand business owners revealed that they felt poor or non-existent follow-up was the biggest stumbling block to the growth of their businesses. Disorganization and inefficient time management ran a close second and third. Lack of follow-up has far reaching impact, including the loss of credibility and trust of clients and prospects alike.

I've Been There

I look back at my early years in a sales position. I was a single mom who was so hungry to be better and do more. I did not finish college, and I knew if I was going to excel to the top I needed to be organized and follow-up. Fortunately, I had some of the greatest mentors who believed in me and helped me realize that it was a whole package, not just one thing, that would help me grow and win! When I failed, I failed BIG. But when I WON, it was so fine! It made me hungry for more.

Now for the Good News

This book was written to shed light on the need for effective follow-up strategies and the means to achieve them. It contains stories of failures and success of real salespeople, business owners and entrepreneurs. They share the reasons that follow-up, or lack of it, played a role in the successes and disappointments of their diverse careers. I'm so appreciative of the time they took to share these stories with me.

The book also provides my insights and advice on making the process of follow-up an integral function of every business transaction, from the first contact to the closing of each deal. It includes examples of the tools I have developed to help turn these processes into habits and space for your own notes and thoughts. I've also provided a companion journal to take with you on calls. It supplies ideas to assist you in developing follow-up processes tailored to meet your own business needs.

Like someone told me years ago, "The tools are as good as the person who takes the initiative to use them." The book is short, so take the time to really reflect on these stories, take some notes, and find yourself a WIN!

In closing, my wish is that by offering you new ideas and helpful tools this book will inspire focus, determination and positive action. These are the magic ingredients that can turn your simplest of thoughts into reality, and help build a momentum that can change your life in amazing ways. No excuses! Follow-up and follow through!

I would love to hear from you with insights and suggestions that have helped fuel your own success and that you'd like me to share with others through my newsletters and blogs.

May you find the "fortune in the follow-up"!

1

Relationships

**"Success blossoms
through the relationships
you build and
the continued help
you give others."**

~ Jean MacDonald ~

What is Your "Secret Sauce" Recipe?

Today, the key to success is to stand out to your customers and prospects – for all the right reasons! First, you need to define what makes you and your business unique in your marketplace. What extras or incentives do you bring to the table that will make prospects or current customers sit up and take notice? What's in the "Secret Sauce" that distinguishes your products or services from those of your competitors?

I share this with you because it's a lesson I learned the hard way. As a young insurance agent, new to the business, I soon became overwhelmed by all the paperwork, calls and contacts that pulled at my attention from all directions. At that early stage of my career, I hadn't learned yet how important organization and establishing a clear sense of direction were to my success. I became buried in business cards and leads, but had no plan or time to follow up on them. Business got done, but just barely, and the only thing that pulled me through that period was a willingness to learn and a tenacious "I can do this" attitude.

Through persistence, little by little I began to make headway in discovering my strengths, and the first ingredient in my secret sauce became my skill at niche marketing. I had begun to identify distinct segments of the business community (manufacturing and transport companies, for example) and found that this targeted marketing approach made the best use of my time and resulted in more sales.

I still had a long way to go in refining my recipe, though, a personal setback knocked me for a loop and caused me to lose focus. I went through a divorce and found myself raising my children alone on a significantly reduced income. Just when I needed increased success the most, I was trapped in a paralyzing slump and struggling to pay the bills. In the ensuing months, the commissions dried up and I lived in fear that I was going to lose everything.

Finding the Fortune

That was when I made a connection that helped to change my life. Trying to turn things around, I had continued to network whenever I could, even if my heart wasn't in it. At one network event, I stood up and gave my 60-second commercial, letting other members know that a good referral for me would be a restaurant owner or manager. Afterward, a few people mentioned that they would be willing to make some introductions. Then a new member approached me. He was a printer who invited me to have coffee the next day to discuss an idea he had.

When we met the next morning, he proceeded to tell me that he represented over 200 restaurants, printing their menus and other marketing materials. My eyes lit up immediately, as I visualized a treasure trove of 200 new leads to sell policies to. He immediately noticed my interest, and his next words were like a splash of cold water on my face. "Whoa there, just a second. Do you think that I'm just going to turn my customer list over to you?" I felt my face flush with embarrassment because, in fact, that is what I had been hoping for.

Sensing my discomfort, he quickly went on to tell me that his idea actually was to invite me to attend an upcoming restaurant association meeting as his guest. He explained that I needed to get involved and become part of the organization, learn all I could about the industry and help to recruit new members. He stressed the importance of becoming known, liked and trusted before trying to make sales.

These new approaches and priorities went on to become key ingredients in my own, personal secret sauce recipe. I accepted his invitation and began immersing myself in understanding the specialized needs of restaurant owners and managers. I practiced the art of helping others, meeting members for coffee, and bringing new members to the organization. Building relationships this way had the added benefit of earning me referrals from new customers from their own industry contacts; my investment of time and effort in building relationships and educating myself began to pay off.

Over a period of several years, I achieved so much more than a fat portfolio of new insurance accounts. I forged new friendships and business alliances, earned the trust of my customers and finally identified all the ingredients in my powerful secret sauce recipe.

As always, effectively following up to serve my customers' needs and cultivate new opportunities was at the top of that ingredient list.

What is your "Secret Sauce" Recipe?

Give some thought to a niche or industry that you can learn about and develop.

_____

_____

_____

_____

_____

_____

_____

_____

_____

_____

"Look for your choices,
pick the best one, then go with it."

~ Pat Riley ~

Making Choices

I find it fascinating to go to a business function or networking event and observe the other people in the room. Some people are interested in food, while others seem to be intent on standing and holding up the walls. Still, others choose to talk only with those they know well or already do business with. Sometimes, though very infrequently, I see those rare individuals who choose to act as hosts, even when they're not.

What do I mean? Let me explain since it's a technique and way of connecting that I like to emulate. When I am a guest at these type of events, I tend to linger near the door, where I can meet and greet newcomers. I want to learn who the regulars are, which people are new to the organization, and most of all get to know those people who have that "spark," that special something that enables them to connect with others and build lasting relationships and alliances.

I also make it my mission to help reserved or nervous newcomers feel welcome and comfortable. We've all been there before, in awkward situations where you're surrounded by people but don't feel part of the group. I make a point of steering clear of the folks who are there strictly for the socializing and food.

We all make choices at these gatherings. Because my time is a valuable commodity, I choose to meet people who also want to build relationships and explore opportunities. The best way to help others become involved is by making good connection choices ourselves.

The choice is yours but after you meet and greet don't forget the Fortune is in the Follow-Up!

"I think a role model is a mentor
- someone you see on a daily basis,
and you learn from them."
~ Denzel Washington ~

Are You Ready for a Mentor?

When you think of the word mentor, what comes to mind? A wise and trusted counselor? An influential and experienced sponsor? Someone who offers support in achieving your goals? A mentor can be all that and more. I know because I have had several mentors in my lifetime. Though in the beginning, I didn't realize the full measure of their value.

Over the years I came to understand that those individuals were more than just friends I could reach out to and talk with when I was down and out. They also listened when I described the obstacles that I perceived to be in my way and (in a supportive and encouraging way) challenged me to be accountable for taking action to overcome the challenges. Their suggestions were drawn from wisdom acquired in meeting their own challenges and each had chosen to become proactive problem solvers to achieve their dreams.

There are potential mentors all around you, so don't wear blinders as you seek them out. Mentors can be found in all vocations and walks of life; some may be up and coming go-getters and others may offer a seasoned perspective acquired through many years of experience. My own mentors range in age from 35 to 75; their fields of expertise are as diverse as their ages.

My "techie" mentor is currently the youngest. He chose to specialize in a wired (and wireless) world that, years earlier, seemed like a foreign country to me. He not only helps me resolve technical issues, but he also teaches me how to expand my knowledge and explore the potential that new technologies offer for my own business needs. In exchange, I am able to mentor him in creating business strategies, using skills drawn from my own experiences; an ideal win-win situation for mentor and mentee.

Another current mentor is a woman I had thought of for many years as simply a good friend until it dawned on me that, when it came to business, she was always frank and honest, giving me straight answers and practical advice. She also knows how to ask just the right questions and then provides guidance in helping me come up with solutions to complete projects or overcome problems. She and I talk at least once a month. She holds me accountable for following through on the issues we've discussed.

Do you feel like it's time to find a mentor or mentors of your own? Are you ready to take the next steps in propelling yourself and your business toward greater success? Are you willing to listen to constructive feedback and advice, to commit and follow through on the action plans a mentor may help you to develop?

These are important questions to ask yourself because a mentor's time is valuable and shouldn't be taken lightly. Know what your goals are in seeking out a mentor and be able to clearly define and express what you are seeking to learn. Have your questions ready. During conversations, take notes if you need to. Otherwise, you are wasting both your mentor's time and your own. Enhance your credibility by being prepared.

Seek out successful people whom you know, like and trust, whose values are in sync with your own. It is an honor to be a mentor and a privilege to be mentored; there needs to be a good fit in order for the relationship to be rewarding for both mentor and mentee.

If it isn't already apparent, follow-up is an integral aspect of a successful mentoring relationship. You can talk about strategies and solutions with the wisest and savviest people in the world, but there's one more step to making your own success a reality. You must follow up with action and a sense of accountability that keeps you moving toward your goal.

Make a list of those you know who could help you on your quest for a great mentor, an accountability partner.

Then think about "why" they would be that special mentor. After you have identified a few, call or set up coffee with them, tell them about the guidance you need. Let them know your intentions and see if they would enjoy working with you.

"Trust is the glue of life.
It's the most essential ingredient
in effective communication.
It's the foundational principle that
holds all relationships."

~ Stephen Covey ~

LinkedIn: Where Business Relationships are Born

When was the last time you looked at your LinkedIn profile?
For many of us, creating a LinkedIn page complete with a professional photo, solid and searchable profile information, and informative links has taken a back seat to building a presence on the "flashier" and highly visible social media platforms: Facebook, Twitter, Instagram etc. But if you're a business professional at any level, from brand new sales associate to entrepreneur to CEO, it's time to expand your social media horizons. For a long time now, LinkedIn has been exactly where the most successful businesspeople have established a presence, connecting with industry peers and long-lost colleagues, as well as current customers and a multitude of brand new prospects.

LinkedIn is here to stay and getting more powerful every day. Be proactive and get started now. Your presence in this dynamic and ever-growing network could be key to the growth of your business. Not quite sure how it all works? Connect with a savvy colleague over coffee or lunch, or get the help of a social media guru. You're sure to find someone who can work within your budget. Try searching that expert on LinkedIn and learn more. On the following page in include some simple and easy-to-follow advice from a social media master, Eddie Soto, CEO of Online Enterprises, Inc. (see LinkedIn: Relationships Matter).

In addition, I recently read a book called *The Art of Social Media: Power Tips for Power Users* by Guy Kawasaki and Peg Fitzpatrick. It is a crash course that will help fast track your social media success.

So what does this have to do with follow-up?
The same rules apply in social media networking as they do to events that you attend in person. When you make a connection, acknowledge it, grow it and strengthen it with the tools that you

already know work best: personal notes and emails, follow up calls and invitations to meet. LinkedIn offers so many other ways to reach out to your audience, including the ability to easily link articles, press releases and industry-related white papers, plus provide information about your current projects and new products or services available. This is accomplished in a non-intrusive, simple and self-contained format. The extra time you invest in regularly updating this social media platform will be well worth your follow-up effort!

"Relationships Matter"

LinkedIn Edit Points:

- Use your full name. Unless you don't wish to be found in search results.

- Clear pictures of faces get best responses, more profile visits and connection requests versus images of buildings, logos, pets, etc…

- LinkedIn is a searchable network; provide lots of company, organization, and project names.

- In edit mode, ensure that you are customizing your URLs for search tracking and directories.

- LinkedIn identifies heavily by profession and industry, so be sure to include keywords that capture your specific product, service, niche and specialty. Be creative and different.

- If you are the CEO, Founder, Owner of your business, include your job title. Like attracts like.

- Request connections and engage early in the workweek during your regions business hours. LinkedIn is relatively quiet during the evenings and weekends.

- In your summary section, you have 2000 characters to tell your visitor all about yourself, use the characters!

- Cross link your Twitter to LinkedIn. Filter tweets to post to LinkedIn by using hashtags #in or #li.

- Reach out to groups and people search to begin building your network. Social etiquette rules apply.

- Take advantage of LinkedIn Answers, LinkedIn Apps, LinkedIn Mobile for lead generations.

- Remember, people read content more than ads so start there. Links to blog posts, articles, press releases, headlines, events all create curiosity, likes, shares and responses.

- Don't be afraid to be human and occasionally share a good joke or story.

"The greatest value you can add
is to become more of yourself."

~ Sally Hogshead ~

Learning About Yourself and Others

Working with different personality styles has always been fascinating to me. The illustration on the following page (DISC Chart) will give you a brief overview of various personality traits, defined in four distinct categories. Individuals may exhibit characteristics across the different groups, depending on circumstances, but generally one set is more dominant than the others in daily life. Based on those dominant traits, almost all of us will fall into one of the four groups. Beneath the illustration are some questions that will help you to better understand yourself, others, and how to work with each personality type.

DISC is a helpful resource in assessing the best way to deal with situations where interpersonal relationships are involved which is nearly all of the time. Different, more specific versions of the assessment can help to anticipate how persons are likely to react when functioning as team members, managers, or in leadership roles. DISC is also useful in helping to determine a course of action when assigning jobs or resolving problems within project teams. (see DISC illustration at end of this story)

Throughout my years of growing and leading successful teams, I've found this simple, one-page chart and the accompanying questions to be an excellent tool for understanding people and getting to know them better. Once you have recognized a person's communication and personality style, it becomes much easier to develop trust and help them to achieve more and become better leaders.

The Fascination Advantage®: Science-Based Personality Brand Measurement

I've recently become a Certified Advisor with a new product called The Fascination Advantage®. You're probably familiar with assessments such as Meyers-Briggs® or Clifton Strengthsfinder, but this is different. This test doesn't measure how you see the world but how the world sees you.

Finding the Fortune

Your personality has one primary advantage: it's how you add value. Now, for the first time, you can measure exactly how your personality adds unique value to your business transactions or branding. It's what makes you different and helps you stand out from the crowd. Think of it as a natural superpower. When you effectively communicate using this advantage, you attract more attention, build stronger relationships, and earn more revenue.

For more information, please visit my website at: www.NetworkConnectSucceed.com/sales-tools

DISC - Working with Different Personalities

"D"	"I"	"S"	"C"
• Dominant	• Inspirational	• Supportive	• Cautious
• Driven	• Influencing	• Submissive	• Competent
• Demanding	• Inducing	• Stable	• Calculating
• Determined	• Impressive	• Steady	• Concerned
• Decisive Doer	• Interactive	• Sentimental	• Careful
• Delegator	• Interest in people	• Shy	• Contemplative

Characteristics

Results-oriented	People-oriented	Family-oriented	Detail oriented
Quick decisions	Loves to talk	Loyal	Perfectionist
Controlling people	Motivational	Slow to change	Critical
Power / Authority	Enthusiastic	Security minded	Analytical
Rule-maker	Recognition oriented	Rule follower	Takes time to change

Communication

Let them talk	Focus on relationship building	You talk most	Don't get too personal
They will tell you what they want	Let them talk	May not ask questions	Answer questions thoroughly
They may not listen to you	Take an interest in them	Focus on flexibility	Build credibility

Benefits Focus

State-of-the-art product	Easy-going	Guarantee	Guarantee
Easy and quick to use	Friends will notice	Flexibility	Flexibility
Big international company	Recognition oriented	Training & support	Training & support
Management	Impact on people	Uncertain economy	Uncertain economy
High Income potential	Friends in company	What is good for family	What is good for family
Independent	Loves attention	Sharing the facts	Sharing the facts

Biggest Root Fear

Being Taken	What others will think	Changing & loss of security	Criticism of work

Questions to understand who they are:

1. **Tell me a little bit about yourself or your situation?**
   - D - Will tell you their Accomplishments?
   - I - Will tell you Who They Know
   - S - Will tell you about their Family
   - C - Will ask you "Why, what do you want to know?"

2. **What do you like most / least about what you do?**

3. **Describe for me the ideal career and lifestyle situation or you if you could have it in the way you want it?**

For more information contact: Jean MacDonald, DTM
Jean@JeanConnects.com
Additional resources available at: www.NetworkConnectSucceed.com/resources
Jean MacDonald © 2017 • All Rights Reserved

It's not about knowing
a lot of people.
It's about knowing a lot
about the
people you know.

~ unknown ~

Doing it for the Right Reason

By Lynn Lionhood

I found the habit of good follow-up to be one of the most important elements to success. I once attended a chamber breakfast about two hours from my office. Being a breakfast event I had to leave very early. Once there, I found it to be a speed networking event which I had never participated in before. This is how it worked: meet ten businesses over your juice and speak for two minutes, then move to the next table; meet ten more businesses over your pastry and speak for two minutes; at the last table, meet ten additional businesses over your entrée and speak for two minutes. Gather your cards, and the event is over. Everyone dispersed very quickly rather than continuing to network.

The following day I reached out to each of the businesses I had met and requested an opportunity to have coffee, breakfast or lunch to learn more about them and their business. One of them responded quickly. I drove about two and a half hours to his office and began a relationship. He spoke again about the company and his three employees. I reached out several more times and as the friendship began he asked if I would like to present my benefits to his three employees. I happily agreed. This was certainly not a money proposition. Because I had done much of the driving to meet with only three employees, I would definitely lose money on this relationship. But I had developed a friendship and knew his three employees were very important to him. I knew they were as important to him as to someone who had hundreds of employees, and I told him this.

After doing the enrollment, I was asked to come to his office. Two and a half hours later he explained how happy they were with the presentation. I thanked him for the opportunity and he asked if I would like to do an enrollment at his other 13 locations with anywhere from 15-18 employees each. I was delighted!

I completed those enrollments and was again requested to come to his office. He explained that everything had gone better than he had expected. I praised him for the enthusiasm with which the managers at each location had welcomed me. They closed the offices for an hour for the lunch I provided and edified me to the employees by explaining they were going to take the benefit themselves because they saw value.

He then asked me if I would like to do an enrollment in Memphis, TN at another of his locations with 400 employees. I was shocked. We arranged all the details and while in Tennessee I asked the manager just how many employees did this company have. I was told they had 14,000!

When I returned to the Chicagoland area, I went to my contact's office and told him that I knew how many employees he had, and I asked why he had not disclosed this the day I had first met him at the chamber breakfast. He explained that if he had told everyone that day, you could be sure that everyone would have been at his doorstep. Because he said he had three employees, I was the only one that contacted him. This told him that I was interested in his company for the right reasons. My continuing to build the relationship before asking for the business again solidified that it was not just going to be about the money.

I have learned to build the relationship first, always do the follow-up, and remember that everyone's business is so very important to them (regardless of the size).

2

Motivation

**Live as if you were
to die tomorrow.
Learn as if you
were to live forever.**

~ Gandhi ~

Finding the Fortune

Are You a Hot Tomato?

It's been said that "nothing happens until somebody sells something." While this may be true, the deeper truth is that building relationships reaps the bigger reward: not just a single sale, but ongoing sales to customers who have come to know and trust you.

My sales journey began one hot August day when I was 10 years old. My family lived in a large housing development with more than 80 homes, so there were plenty of kids to hang out with. We'd get together beneath one of the big shade trees, having fun dreaming up things to do. We all liked the idea of having more spending money. One day we decided that opening our own lemonade stand would be a good way to raise some money. We were sure all the neighbors would be happy to pay us for a nice, cold drink on warm summer days. We'd have fun and make money at the same time.

Fired up, I raced home to tell my mom about our plan. Dad was just coming in the door and we walked in the house together, as I chattered excitedly about my new business venture. I could tell he was pleased that I wanted to become a young entrepreneur. We found mom in the kitchen, even busier than usual with the annual tomato canning ritual. My father was renowned in the neighborhood for his big, juicy beefsteak tomatoes (he'd even won awards for size, color, and taste) and mom was at the countertop, surrounded by a sea of ripe, red tomatoes ready to be packed in large, glass mason jars.

She listened as Dad and I sat at the table and talked about my business plan. After a few moments, he nodded thoughtfully, and then said to me, "I want you to sit here for a few minutes and think about this project. You know that the other kids are going to be doing the same thing. You'll all be trying to sell the same product. That's sure to cut into your sales. Can you think of another approach, a different idea?"

He could tell I wasn't quite getting his drift, so he made another suggestion. "Sit here and look around you for a few minutes. See if you can come up with something." With that, he got up from his chair and told me he'd be back soon to find out what I came up with.

I did as he said, sitting quietly at the table looking around me, while mom busied herself with the canning. Then it struck me; I could sell dad's tomatoes! We always had an overabundance, so many that we'd end up having to give them away. Why not sell them instead; people were always asking for them and would happily pay for something that delicious.

By the time dad came back in the kitchen, I was fired up and ready to begin my entrepreneurial career. He was smart; he knew that if he left me alone to think of a product solution myself, I would take ownership of the idea and run with it. Once that happened, he supported me all the way. We prepared by giving my red wagon a new coat of paint to deliver my product, bought a receipt book and a bag to hold my money. That summer's business venture was a huge success. Everyone loved dad's tomatoes, and I even expanded my offerings to include his cucumbers and carrots as well.

At the end of the season dad asked me, "***What do you need to do next?***" Not knowing the answer, I asked for his advice. He went on to explain that now was the time to prepare for the upcoming season, gathering the neighbors' names and addresses and staying in touch with them. He even suggested that I send them handwritten notes thanking them for their business and letting them know I would be back next year. My dad taught me a very valuable lesson that summer. Make people feel important by following up and letting them know I would return to do business with them again.

Think about things you learned as a child.

Did you learn lessons then that you can use today to help you with your follow-up?

"The more I practice, the luckier I get."
~ Arnold Palmer ~

No Laughing Matter

By Ellen Schnur

Follow-up can be defined in lots of ways: the salesperson who writes a personal thank you note to each prospect after a call; the doctor who contacts his patients a few days after visits to check on their progress; the colleague who quickly responds with budget numbers after a meeting. In my case, follow-up was the key that helped me to realize my dreams.

I had joined an improv comedy group in the Chicago area and been attending rehearsals for about two months. I enjoyed learning and performing improv more than anything I had ever done. I would laugh so hard I would go home with my sides aching. I was offered the chance to be part of their next improv show. The director and the rest of the team assured me that I was more than ready and that the experience would be lots of fun. I was nervous, but boosted by their confidence, I decided to go for it. After all, rehearsals went well, and I assumed the show would be more of the same.

The night of the performance, attendance was standing room only. Shortly before we went on, the entire cast gathered in a back room, energized by the full house. I had invited family and friends to attend my debut appearance and was excited that they were out there in the crowd.

And then the show started. I realized very quickly that I really had no idea what I was doing and that things were not going well, at least on my part. The rest of the cast was terrific, and they carried me along, but by the end of the show, I was horrified. What had I been thinking, inviting so many to watch me fumble up on stage?

After the show, I lingered backstage longer than the rest of the cast. Luckily, when I emerged the bar was still full, and with seating scarce and a long wait for drinks, my friends had left. I spied my husband at the bar, slid in beside him and ordered a martini (I rarely drink martinis!). We were both quiet for a few moments. Finally, I said, "I was terrible tonight." He said nothing, and as the seconds ticked by I became more upset. "That's it. I quit. I should not be doing this." His response? "Okay."

His acceptance triggered something in me, and my embarrassment turned into fury. Shaken by its intensity I couldn't speak for a few moments, but then I had a startling revelation. "Wait a minute, " I thought. "Screw everyone else! I've never loved doing anything more than this. I'm not going to give it up." I took a swig of my martini, turned to my husband and said, "That's it. I'm taking classes at Second City."

On my first day of class at the renowned comedy theater's training center, I was terrified. Surrounded by mostly male twenty-somethings, I eyed the door numerous times, wondering if I should head out and just keep going. With each class, the fear gradually became replaced by so many moments of absolute joy that I stuck with it and ended up completing the whole improv program.

So what does this have to do with follow-up? Four years later I own my own company and teach applied improv workshops. The reason I am able to do what I love is because I kept following up on my own passion. I kept following up on what I loved doing, despite my fear. I kept going, and today I help others conquer their fears and follow their passions.

The Lost Art of Networking

People can't do business with you if they don't know you.

Did you know that 75% of all small business sales come from referrals generated through business owners networking? Yet, many businesspeople don't understand how effective networking works and how to leverage its impact in building successful, long-lasting business relationships. Surprisingly, many of those same owners would vigorously maintain that they act as ambassadors for their businesses, but most never leave their embassies to expand out into the community. Imagine the untapped potential. Networking is a powerful tool that is too often underutilized and misunderstood. Effective outreach is the optimum way to build your network and your business.

Becoming an effective, productive networker doesn't have to consume all your time or resources. A simple change in your mindset can give you new "networking clarity." Adopt networking as a way of life, developing and projecting an attitude of engagement with everyone you meet. You can expand your network by simply becoming aware of the people you encounter every day, in business settings or when running errands. One of my most successful business relationships began as I stood waiting in line for a cup of coffee at Dunkin' Donuts. See every person you meet as a potential connection – the person in front of you at the grocery store could be your next business prospect. Kick-start your success simply by allocating a little more time to "being seen."

"You need to dig your well before you are thirsty."
Harvey McKay, businessman and bestselling author

Begin laying the groundwork right now by meeting and connecting with the people in your own community. That step alone will go an amazingly long way in bringing you the business success that eludes so many people who don't understand or value the art of networking. Open up, engage and make connections that turn into customers for life. Start by inviting the people you meet to have coffee and get to know them; talk about the possibilities. Those follow-up cups of coffee can be the start of relationships that will take you on the business success ride of your life! (See the coffee conversation questions in Chapter 7).

Networking "Know-How"

From Jean MacDonald

Take the Tools:

- ☐ Name Badge
- ☐ Business Cards
- ☐ Pens
- ☐ Brochures

Set a Goal:

- ☐ Number of People to Meet
- ☐ Attainable
- ☐ Don't Leave Until Goal is Met

Be a Host:

- ☐ Offer to Greet Others at Door
- ☐ Introduce Self
- ☐ Introduce the Contact to Someone Else

Engage Your Ears:

- ☐ Listen First
- ☐ Ask Questions
- ☐ Tell What You Do (in 10 seconds or less)

Develop a Relationship:

- ☐ Do Not Sell
- ☐ Find a Personal Connection

Make Referrals:

- ☐ Give First
- ☐ Then Receive

Collect Cards:

- ☐ Keep 1, Pass 1 on as a Referral
- ☐ Give Them Your Card

Time Development:

- ☐ Place Business Cards in a Contact List
- ☐ Schedule "Cup of Coffee" Meeting to Build Relationship

Build Relationship

- ☐ Be Disciplined

Follow Up:

- ☐ Make Notes on Back of Card
- ☐ Within 2 Days Write a Note, Place a Call, Send an Email
- ☐ Set Another Point of Contact

Jean@JeanConnects.com • www.NetworkConnectSucceed.com/resources

The Coffee Triangle

Time is one of your most valuable assets and meeting for coffee or lunch with power partners, clients and prospective clients requires a lot of it. But the stronger your relationships are, the more your credibility is enhanced, which leads to the referrals that are so important to the health and growth of every business.

Your investment of time is so significant that I came up with a way to manage that time and build those strong relationships. I call it "The Coffee Triangle" and it works this way:

- You take the lead as the inviter and choose two people you want to introduce to each other. You may know them both well, or perhaps you know one and want to get to know the other. Try to select two people whose outlook and personalities you feel will complement each other (and you), to determine if there is a synergy between the three of you. This compound effect can result in good business and quality information and resources for everyone.

- You will be steering the meeting and will want to follow the simple format of making the introductions, fielding the questions (see Coffee Conversation Questions in Chapter 7) and then summarizing with a quick overview of your discussion at the end of the meeting. This will help to keep the dialogue going, which can result in future meetings and the possibility of making new "limousine partners" (see the example in Chapter 3).

- Throughout your meeting, listen well to both of the other parties, remember to take good notes and star those items that you think are of most interest to the three of you. Focus on talking about these, and identify information and resources that can be shared. There is power in numbers when people who are in sync get together and create a bridge that allows for the free exchange of knowledge that will benefit each attendee. Everyone should be encouraged to follow up as soon as possible with shared information.

In fact, timely and efficient follow-up should always be at the top of the list in all of your meetings and transactions. Combined with this powerful relationship-building technique, the benefits to your business will be amazing!

Coffee Triangle

Credibility

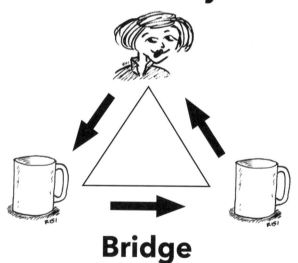

Bridge

Jean MacDonald, DTM
Jean@JeanConnects.com • www.NetworkConnectSucceed.com
Jean MacDonald © 2017 • All Rights Reserved

Follow Up That Was So Sweet

by Eddie Soto

Four years ago at a business expo, participating on a panel made up of experts in a number of fields, I was asked to present on the subject of social media marketing to a group of small business owners. Afterwards one of the attendees, an owner of a local confectionery store, came up to ask me some additional questions.

He told me he had thought his business had a good local following, with core customers who came in at least weekly, plus the local high school and college crowd. However, after hearing me speak, he began to think there was a whole untapped community out there that he wasn't reaching; including younger kids, families, and more. While he had a basic website and a small presence on social media, his LinkedIn profile was just a shell. He also acknowledged that he wasn't very familiar with online language, functionality and the profile features that could be used on social media.

We scheduled a series of meetings and I showed him how, with just a little effort, he could really expose his business to many more people. I helped him build social media channels, including a LinkedIn profile, that were relevant, compelling and offered inviting images and stories. We captured testimonials, created a series of giveaway promotions, conducted surveys, and created "call to action" posts. I also introduced him to several industry-specific online discussion groups.

Thanks to this sound commitment to working on his LinkedIn page and other social media sites, plus his engagement with online community groups, his business grew 150% in the first year. Four years later he has seen prolific growth in his online presence, experiencing an increase of 700% in his network followers resulting in big improvements in business traffic and a corresponding increase to his bottom line!

By following up to engage with a new online community through LinkedIn and other social outlets, he brought value and benefit to his customers, and achieved a new level of success. A viral buzz was created, that led to recommendations and introductions and raised awareness of his business throughout his target market.

Are you motivated to develop your network?

What content can you bring to engage, inform, invite, educate and stimulate your community to respond to your call to action? See the LinkedIn illustration in Chapter 1 with some simple ideas that can get you started.

"Time to Plan"

3

Strategy

**"Meeting Once is Nice,
Twice is Great,
Building Relationships,
Priceless!"**
~ Jean MacDonald ~

Finding the Fortune

Dressing for the Part

As a young woman, I learned how much making a good first impression has to do with creating the opportunity for good follow-up. I owe it all to my mother. You see, when I was growing up one of the first things Mom taught me was that it doesn't matter how much money you have, you should always dress as well as you can, wearing neatly pressed clothes, with shoes polished and a pulled-together, organized look.

Her advice paid off when I was hired as the newest and youngest agent at a New Jersey insurance agency. It was during the era of "dress down Fridays," when employees could come to the office wearing jeans and tee shirts instead of their regular business attire. I wasn't comfortable with the notion then or now, and my concession to dressing down was showing up in a black sweater dress instead of my usual suit, with a simple strand of pearls and shining black heels.

I was sitting at my desk making phone calls when the boss stuck his head of his office and called to me, "Yo, kid. I've got a meeting I can't make this morning. You're the only one dressed for a call, so take the application and go see the client." Being the new kid on the block, I was floored that he asked me to stand in for him. On the other hand, because I was dressed to do business, I felt confident that I could go out and represent the agency well.

Off I went, papers in hand, to meet the potential client. I had no clue how big this piece of business might be, but the prospect was a very large trucking company. I met with the client, helped him complete the application, and then brought everything back to the office so we could pull a quote together. He had seemed quite impressed with my readiness and demeanor. I had gathered all the details needed to set up an account. Being new, I hadn't had the answers for all of the client's questions, but with the help of my boss, I gathered the additional information he had asked for.

Finding the Fortune

The following week we went out to present our proposal. Once again, I was neatly dressed and ready with the promised follow-up information. Together, we closed the deal that day, marking the largest account I had written so far and the start of a very successful insurance career.

The door to that good fortune was opened by being dressed to succeed. It was the key to entering a whole new world of business opportunities, each requiring the essential follow-up that ensures sustained growth and continued success.

Are You Interested in Being Interesting?

I heard a quote from my son the other day: "Are you interested in being interesting?" Though I wasn't sure where he had picked it up, it made me pause and think about the prospect I was on my way to meet for coffee.

Many times when we meet new people, our tendency is to jump in at the first opening in the conversation and offer up our own thoughts and ideas. That's common and happens countless times a day. I reflected that I had also recently heard it said that a better ratio is, "Five minutes of listening, to one minute of talking." Interesting!

That really makes sense. When you spend more time listening to what the other person is saying, expressing sincere interest by giving them your full attention, you're far more likely to be able to ask smart questions and contribute relevant knowledge of your own. Practicing this listening technique also helps to avoid the pitfall of missing half of what the speaker is saying because you are already thinking ahead to what you want to express.

Other people can tell when you are truly interested and listening fully to them and that engagement makes you more interesting in their eyes. You gain credibility through sincerity and by reinforcing your interest with both verbal and non-verbal gestures: smiling, eye contact, your posture, and mirroring will all encourage the other person to be at ease and continue. The speaker knows that you are interested and will communicate more easily, openly and honestly. It is human nature to want to reciprocate, so when you do speak it is much more likely that person will extend you the same courtesy that you showed to him or her.

When you are at ease with each other, the exchange of ideas and knowledge is much more productive, often leading to a new sale, an endorsement or a referral. So starting today, make this your mantra for every conversation you have: **Are you interested in being interesting!**

Want to Score Big? Follow-Up Counts

By Jim Mecir

Bases were loaded with no outs, and we were winning by a run when I got the call to the bullpen. It was a bleak situation and to make matters worse, we were playing the powerful New York Yankees. Even if I didn't give up a hit, it was possible I could give up two runs if their outs advanced base runners. Resigned to the fact it might happen, I just wanted to get enough outs to stop a big inning.

I stepped on the pitching mound and delivered one strike, then another and another. Strike three, one out! I felt a little bit of confidence seeping through the gloom. The next hitter stepped in the box and I did the improbable, three more consecutive strikes for another strikeout. What once was an impossible situation was turning into a manageable one. My confidence was at an all-time high, and I had this unbelievable adrenaline rush. I felt like I couldn't be stopped!

Then I was stopped. The umpire called timeout. I guessed that the Yankees hoped to disrupt my momentum and were trying to "ice me down." Turned out I was dead wrong because as I glanced to my right, I saw my own pitching coach walking out to the mound.

This had to be a bad dream. I had just struck out two hitters on six pitches. I had momentum and great confidence. Didn't my coach realize what he was doing by breaking that rhythm? He stepped up to the mound and said, "I just want to make sure we're still on the same page." My catcher and I answered him with more than a touch of exasperation. He then returned to the dugout, and I got back up on the mound, but something was different. My confidence, composure and momentum had dissolved. I had been iced down by my own coach in the closing moments of a crucial inning.

The next hitter stepped up to the plate. We battled for a couple of pitches, and then he hit a soft fly ball down the right field line. It landed one foot inside the foul line. All three runs scored and the hitter ended up on second base. Our one run lead turned into a two run deficit that would prove to be insurmountable.

Would the result have been different if the coach hadn't come out to the mound? There was no way to know for sure, but one thing was certain: there had been a critical communication gap. The coach, pitching staff and catchers had met before the game to ensure that we were "all on the same page." There was ample time before that inning to follow-up and make sure we still had the same strategy. I had erred in assuming that my coach knew my plan. We cannot make assumptions about what information team members have. Have you ever assumed that your team was on the same page but in reality, they weren't even reading the same book?

As a professional, you would like to think you can overcome a mistake like that, but in sports, as in life, momentum and confidence are extremely important commodities. Effective follow up goes hand in hand with the intangible assets of leadership and effective communication which are essential to the successful outcome of any situation.

"It is such an honor to work with Jim Mecir. He has just been inducted into the New York State Baseball Hall of Fame, November 2016." - Jean MacDonald

Limousine Thinking

Take a look at the illustration that accompanies this chapter. It represents two choices that can make all the difference in the world to your business success.

Riding the bus is something we've all done to get where we're going. It's quick and practical, gets you from Point A to Point B, but beyond that, you're pretty much just along for the ride. People get on and off at different destinations, but we don't really get to know them beyond the occasional nod and smile. The bus ride is the equivalent of attending a crowded networking event, where you may have enough time to exchange a few words and business cards, but not much chance for meaningful conversation.

The limousine ride—now that's another story. You take a limo for special, significant occasions, and you choose the people who will accompany you with care. People you know well or want to know better, individuals who are headed for the same destination, who won't be hopping off somewhere along the way.

Think of your fellow passengers in the limo as the carefully chosen VIPs of a mastermind group. These are the business people or professionals you want to learn from and share ideas with. They are experts in their respective fields, who can offer guidance and advice when you encounter challenges. And you, in turn, can offer them the benefit of your own experience and insights. By associating and regularly meeting with these other carefully chosen VIPs you turn a casual bus ride into a productive limo journey toward your business success.

Consider this as you plan your upcoming weeks and months. Balance your bus rides and your limo rides to leverage your time to best advantage. Of course you'll still attend networking events, but make an effort to schedule a breakfast or lunch meeting with your limo group on a bi-weekly or monthly basis. Make the best

Choose the ride of your life!

Your aim isn't to find prospects, although that might happen. It isn't about connecting with people who will grow your business, except perhaps indirectly. Instead it's about people you can help by enriching their lives—and people who might be able to help you if you ask the right questions.

– Chris Brogan

Jean MacDonald, DTM
Jean@JeanConnects.com
www.NetworkConnectSucceed.com

Network Connect Succeed

Bus or Limousine?
it is your choice

Who are your VIP 's along for the ride?

- People you personally want to help succeed.
- People you feel can help you succeed.
- People you care about who could use the help of people you know.

use of time by focusing on goal setting, identifying challenges and solutions, and holding each other accountable for previous action items. Then be sure to close by exchanging referrals, setting the next date (I recommend the same day and time), make a commitment to all action items and end on a positive reenforcement of how you appreciate being part of the group. Napoleon Hill said, " A mastermind alliance is built of two or more minds working actively together in perfect harmony toward a common definite object."

In Jack Canfield's book, *The Success Principles* he defines a mastermind planning guide. This guide gives you the tools to assemble your mastermind group. For more information you can also find this valuable information at www.jackcanfiled.com.

Write down the names of potential mastermind partners, check your calendar, and invite them to your first "limo" meeting. It will be well worth the effort, and you're in for the ride of your life!

Your follow through and follow-up starts now.

_____

_____

_____

_____

_____

_____

_____

_____

_____

"Before you read the next few pages does anyone need to check their email?"

~ Anonymous Millennial ~

Motivating Millennial Thinking

By Zachary Slade

As a Millennial in sales and leadership, it's challenging to determine whose methods one should implement. I've heard several people tell me "having any method is better than having no method at all." I firmly believe that statement to be true. However, while sales and leadership methodologies can vary greatly based on the systems used, there are a few time-tested foundational components that hold true across industry and generation. These concepts are often misunderstood by millennials resulting in missed opportunities and limited potential. You'll find that great follow-up is an underlying theme of all five concepts…..

#1 Get Back to Basics

I recently heard a seasoned sales professional tell me, "In order to outsell your competition you need to 'outsmart' your competition." This statement can be applied several ways; all of which are probably true. In the era of electronic communications and quick response expectations, don't forget the human element. Think of simple and effective ways to engage with the emotions of everyone you're dealing with. This will be what creates a connection and differentiates you in the mind of others. Inevitably, creating the excitement for someone to 'want' to talk when you do follow-up.

#2 Stick to It

Remember that loyalty is valued especially by those from prior generations. Whether it's your career, a hobby, or new sales method; mastery takes time and doesn't happen overnight. I believe that, from a young age, we have been trained to not only 'want,' but more devastatingly, 'expect' things immediately. Our experience with technology has reinforced this mental habit by continuously getting faster (meaning 'better') and more advanced (meaning 'easier'). However, we need not confuse virtual expectations with necessary real life process. If we're always searching for 'fast and easy' we'll never reap the fruits of our efforts because we'll always be leaving prior to the harvest.

#3 Age Doesn't Matter

I realize that's a bold statement that, by many accounts, is not true. To clarify, for millennials, I believe that age matters about as much as you'd like it to. People obviously value the knowledge that comes with experience; however, they do not require experience as a necessary component of knowledge. I've met many millennials who have exceptional relationships with clients from all generations. Those individuals are the ones who surround themselves with mentors, coaches, and others who they can actively learn from.

More often than not, when it appears someone is being influenced by age what they're really being influenced by is credibility. Experience increases credibility. However, nothing influences credibility more than leadership ability. The best way to create credibility is to take on a leadership role.

If you are passionate about a specific cause take the initiative to get involved. It's likely that you'll get back more than what you give. I've been active in a local non-profit for a little over a year. The people I've met through the organization have become close friends, mentors, and strategic partners. I firmly believe that the greatest people are the ones whose primary focus is giving back. If you want to become a better person, then surround yourself with those types of people.

#4 Thank You is an Art

A sincere thank you delivered in a unique way is an incredible differentiator. The immediate thought is sending a well-written thank you email after a good meeting. It is because everyone sends an email that a personal note is that much more effective. Take it one step further. How about sending a sincere thank you note just for having a good meeting? I recently had an old friend of mine send me a thank you note for buying him a beer at a bar. Regardless of one's reasoning behind their intention, it's the sincerity that is remembered.

At its core, the art of "thank you" is purely reflected by the creativity in one's eagerness to appreciate the actions of another. It's because of genuine appreciation that individuals will contribute more. People strive for appreciation and the more creative you can make it the better the effect.

#5 Position Yourself Effectively

Around the time the first edition of this book was published I'd asked Jean MacDonald to assist me in the launch of a Business Networking International chapter called The Platinum Rule Network. Since then, we've quickly been recognized as one of the fasted growing and most respected chapters in the region. Jean was someone with experience launching successful chapters and was willing to help me create the chapter that I envisioned.

At the time, I knew very little about formal networking. It was my ability to surround myself with other like-minded and trusted professionals that ultimately lead to our success. However, without someone who has been there before guiding us, it never would have come to fruition. This is a prime example of taking on responsibilities that force an increase in leadership ability. Effective positioning and consistent follow-up used together can create great influence.

"Leaders are made, they are not born. They are made by hard effort, which is the price which all of us must pay to achieve any goal that is worthwhile."

~ Vince Lombardi ~

Leading with Follow-up

by Howard Prager

As leaders, we focus on getting the work done and meeting the growth and development of our business and the people within our organization. A key to this is **follow-up** – making sure that you, your team, your colleagues, even your boss, do what they are committed to or are assigned to work on.

Years ago, I was a leader of a musical combo in high school. I got a call to play a gig for the Knights of Columbus at Techny Cemetery. I was excited, though it seemed like a strange place for a gig. But I was young, naïve, and assumed that maybe there was a nice grassy area near the front of the cemetery where we could play. Upon receipt of my contract, (my only form of follow-up at the time pre-email, texting, etc.) my client called me quite concerned. We weren't playing at Techny Cemetery (which may not even exist) but at Techny *Seminary!* I was happy to find we were playing at a more "lively" venue. Communication, and ensuring you are listening and repeating back, is always important. Lesson learned, no harm done.

Later, when I worked in Executive Education, I managed a program that sent faculty out of town to teach classes on occasion. Imagine my consternation when I got an early call from a client in Buffalo asking where the faculty was? I found out that the faculty had gone to the airport the afternoon before, but the flight was canceled. They had made no effort to contact the client or me to let us know they weren't going to make it! And, they didn't arrange for another flight to even get in the next day. I sure didn't see that coming! It was hard work with short notice, but I managed to get other faculty there to cover the material, and I was able to retain the client. After that, I always make sure to follow-up to ensure the faculty arrives when and where they are supposed to. I also advise them to try not to take the last flight of the day, allowing some wiggle room if a problem should arise – we all know what travel is like. And I never made that mistake again.

I once had a meeting scheduled with a prospect that was a 3-4 hour drive from my office. I left a little early to give myself plenty of time to get there. Only once I arrived, I was surprised to discover the person I was supposed to meet with was sick that day and not in the office. They didn't contact me at all, but I didn't confirm with them our meeting. Now I always follow up and confirm meetings the day before, and I provide my cell number in case there are any problems.

One of the "trickiest" follow-ups is with your boss. I once had a boss who always gave travel assignments at the last minute. That often led to much higher-priced tickets and a frantic rearrangement of schedules. I learned to anticipate travel by following up with the boss about upcoming seminars and meetings I'd heard about through the grapevine. That way, I was able to arrange my schedule to accommodate travel, should I be assigned to attend.

Those are just a few examples of my follow-up success – and not quite success.

I know follow-up can sometimes be seen as nagging or micromanaging. But, if it's done in the right way, follow-up can save you time, embarrassment, frustration, and perhaps impress your client, boss, etc. and win you a new project or client.

What project is sitting on your desk that needs attention?

Follow-up and follow through!

"Clarity Creates Simplicity"

4

Clarity

The Vision of Today is the Abundance of Tomorrow.
~ Jean MacDonald ~

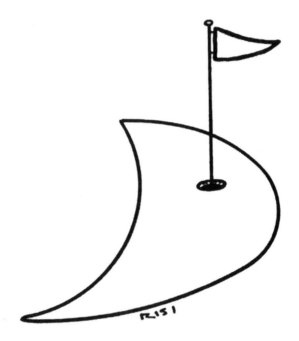

A Golf Lesson

As all golfers know, good follow-through is essential to success in the sport. In this instance, some good follow-up would have made the game even more memorable.

Years ago on a summer day, I arrived in Mount Snow, Vermont, to take golf lessons. I was fortunate to be paired up with a gal who was an even worse golfer than I was. It was inevitable we would hit it off; as we got to know each other, we discovered we were both from New Jersey and, to seal the deal, we were both employed in the insurance industry. We were paired up over the course of two hot, sunny days and she even spared me from sunburn by sharing a small tube of very effective lotion she carried with her. When the weekend was over, we both promised to stay in touch and get together again back in New Jersey. As is often the case, our work schedules and family commitments sidetracked us, and that never happened.

A couple of months later, in early September, my daughter Laura came home from school very excited. Her first math class project was to select and run her own fictitious business, and she was eager to get started. I was happy she asked for my input and advice but suggested to her that we find a business that was a little more fun than insurance. She agreed, and the very next day I happened to attend a networking meeting where I met a successful Mary Kay Cosmetics independent sales director. Thinking this might be a fun venture for Laura and I to work on together, I told my new acquaintance about it, and she agreed. She was kind enough to invite me over to learn more about the products, and I was impressed. Laura was even more excited when I told her about them. We dove in and had a great time working on the project. Little did I know then how this school assignment would impact my own life.

The experience of working with Mary Kay products inspired me to become an independent beauty consultant. I began attending weekly meetings and growing my own team. I soon became a team leader, and when our sales director informed us that Mary Kay would be speaking in person at a company event in New York City in November, we were all thrilled to attend.

As we waited in our auditorium seats for Mary Kays' appearance, imagine my surprise when my summer golfing partner came walking up the aisle. She looked at me, as surprised as I was and asked, "What are you doing here?" I explained that I was a new team leader and that my companions were all my team members. A crestfallen look appeared on her face. "I only needed one more member on our team to earn our first car," she said. "I never even thought of asking you."

Talk about your missed opportunities. Had she put her own labels on the sunscreen samples she shared with me on the golf course, I would have asked her more about them, which would have led to learning about Mary Kay products. She then told me she never thought of bringing up the benefits of joining the business, because she assumed that as the owner of a successful insurance agency, I wouldn't be interested. Just think, simply following up by tagging those lotion samples could have meant substantial financial rewards for her and her team. The upside for me was that I went on to lead a top team, earning not one but several pink Cadillacs.

The story doesn't end there, though. Some years later, I looked her up on LinkedIn, curious to see how she was doing. I discovered she was working as a realtor and living in North Carolina. It so happened that we were interested in some property there, so I contacted her immediately. We reminisced for a bit about our last meeting, and she told me that while she still loved the products, she was no longer involved much in the Mary Kay business.

She went on to tell me she loved the real estate business, especially helping people to find their dream homes. I told her what we were looking for, when we would be in the area and that we would like to meet and learn more. Sounding pleased, she promised to get back to me with information and to confirm the date. I emailed her my contact information and then waited for a follow-up call that never came. We did go to North Carolina as planned, but met with another realtor who answered our questions, followed up with everything we requested. This led to the purchase of the property and building our new home. The fortune is certainly in the follow-up.

When was the last time you promised to make a call or send an email

– and then didn't follow through with the follow-up?

_____

_____

_____

_____

_____

_____

_____

_____

"It was character that got us out of bed, commitment that moved us into action, and discipline that enabled us to follow through"

~ Zig Ziglar ~

Redneck Regret

By Dobie Maxwell

Many years ago while I was in the beginning stages of my standup comedy career, I worked with a southern gentleman who had nothing but complimentary things to say about my comedic ability. We were nearing the end of a week-long engagement at a comedy club in suburban Detroit. He asked if he could buy me lunch the following day because he had an idea brewing in his brain and wanted my honest input. I was an opening act; "buy you lunch" was all I needed to hear.

I showed up the following day and immediately saw he had already invested considerable time and effort into his idea. He had a spiral notebook along with an ample supply of 3x5 index cards. He was visibly excited about sharing his idea. His interest piqued mine, and we ordered lunch.

Halfway through my hamburger, he could wait no longer. He opened his notes and explained a joke formula he wanted to use as the basis of an entire concept. He said he was sure it was going to be hugely successful and he thought I would make an excellent member of the writing team.

"Here's my idea," he said confidently, as I continued to make history of my free hamburger.

"You might be a redneck if…is the setup. Then we fill it in with as many jokes as we can."

"That's IT?" I said, less than impressed.

"Well, kind of" he replied. "I noticed we're working at a comedy club in a bowling alley and they have valet parking. This is Michigan, not Mississippi. There are rednecks everywhere, and I think this is going to be HUGE! I would love it if you came on board and wrote jokes with me."

Trying to break it to him as delicately as I could, between bites of my burger I said to Jeff Foxworthy, "Buddy, no offense but I think this is the dumbest idea I've ever heard. You're a really nice guy, but you asked for my honest opinion, and that's it. This is a gimmick right out of Mad magazine."

Jeff's eyes widened, and he said "I beg to differ. This is going to make me a million dollars!"

That's when I got in his face, and openly mocked him. "A million dollars! A million dollars!"

We finished out our week and had a wonderful time. We even ended up bowling a few games together. From there, Jeff went on to make FAR more than the million dollars he predicted and I went on to a journeyman's career telling jokes to double-digit crowds for the next three decades.

Jeff was and is one of the nicest people I have ever worked with and a hilarious comedian. He has earned every bit of his success. Once in a while we still cross paths. We laugh a lot about Detroit… but he always laughs a lot harder than I do. How hard would it have been to do some simple follow-up, just keep in touch with Jeff and write a few jokes like he asked? Instead, success found me, and I rejected it.

Clarity

"Whatever we plant in our
subconscious mind and nourish
with repetition and emotion
will one day become a reality."
~ Earl Nightingale ~

Repetition, Repetition, Repetition:
A Power Tip To Command Attention and Conquer More Sales

By Andy Horner

If you had to capture the attention of everyone inside a grocery store, how would you do it? Would you yell "FIRE" at the top of your lungs? Knock over a shelf stacked high with glass bottles? Enter with Justin Bieber riding piggy back?

No. You get your seven year old, five year old and three year old sons, with their identical blonde haircuts, to each push one of those kid-sized grocery carts in a line behind you. Then, you lead them down each aisle as you casually shop and push your one year old son in a stroller. At least that's how my wife did it last week. Every customer and employee stopped to say "hello" and comment on the little boy parade. She might as well have been the President of the United States of America.

Besides the cute kid factor, why did it work?

The Principle of Repetition. You can use this principle to build your brand, fill your events, grow your following, market your products, and most importantly - grow your sales. Let me say that again. You can use the Principle of Repetition to grow your sales!

Repetition is a primary element of design, architecture, music, art and nature. In the noisy world of business, repetition of form, sight, sound, smell, touch and sensation conveys meaning and alerts the brain that something important, intelligent and impressive is present.

Repetition is an underused strategy to channel your customer's attention where you want it, on you!

9 Techniques to Apply the Principle of Repetition:

1. Repetition in Public Speaking. When you arrive at a key idea in your speech, state it twice. The second time, say it slowly with added emphasis. This age-old technique improves attentiveness and memory retention.

2. Repetition in Slide Presentations. Write your most pivotal point on a single slide three times. Use a double return between the identical phrases. You'll only need to say it once. Your words will resound in your audience's head three times.

3. Repetition in Product Promotion. When Apple launches a new iPhone, they usually photograph three or four together to create a power image. Follow their lead by displaying your products side-by-side on your website, brochure, white paper, banner ad, or product slick.

4. Repetition in Subject Lines. Subject lines with the same word three times get opens. For instance, if I emailed this article to you, it would carry the subject line, "Repetition, Repetition, Repetition." You would open it.

5. Repetition in Email Messages. Include the call to action in your email two or three times. Add it as a link or bolded text in the body of your message, on a line by itself and again in your closing. Now that your calls to action are no longer overlooked expect clicks and replies to spike.

6. Repetition Disruption. If attention can be triggered by repetition, breaking the pattern can heighten it even more. Picture an ad with a lineup of vacuums that all appear similar, except for the distinctive design of the yellow Dyson. Disruption can draw focus. Use it to distinguish yourself from your competitors in a series of product images, testimonials, or result statistics.

7. Repetition in Follow-Up. After you visit a prospect, send them a follow up email the same day. Use OutStand.com (formerly known as Ace of Sales) - it makes it fast, fun, and creative. Offer an idea or highlight a connection you made during your sales visit. If you don't hear back right away, follow up the next day. Don't nudge. Simply say, "here's another idea" or "another solution came to mind." Frequently, prospects will read your email and think, "When I get back to my desk, I'll respond." But they get distracted and forget. Repetition prompts response.

8. Repetition in Sales Calls. Among the most effective closing techniques in overcoming a final objection is to ask, "If I can guarantee [blank], will you buy from me?" At this point, a customer will often repeat their concern at length. Simply reply, "The answer is yes" and then repeat your question. "If I can guarantee [blank], will you buy from me?" You're focusing them with repetition to make a commitment. It's a bold and confident move that can help win their respect and seal the deal. It applies to phone calls too.

9. Repetition in Branding. A key to branding is to repeat the same message over and over and over and over and over. You may become bored of your logo, positioning statement, and customer promise but if it's working, don't change it. You'll risk losing years of branding equity, and you'll confuse customers.

Bonus Tip: Repetition in Advertisement. Examine a public bulletin board where locals post their ads. Which fliers stand out? The ones with multiple ads stapled side-by-side. Music groups and bands use this practice when they plaster telephone poles with their album art and gig posters. The next time you buy a half-page ad in a local magazine, design your ad a third as wide and repeat it 3 times. See if your ROI goes up.

For more information on repetition in follow-up,
go to: www.outconnecting.com.

"Wise men speak because they have something to say; Fools because they have to say something."

~ Plato ~

Communication for Success

By Leslie Lipps

Communication is the foundation for building relationships both professionally and personally. The more effectively you can communicate with those around you, the more effective YOU are. Focus on these 10 tips to improve and leverage your communication skills.

Here are the top 10 tips:

10. Choose the right tool
Communicating in today's environment is easy! In person, a phone call, send an email, mail a letter or simply text. Each tool and communication option has benefits. If you are sending follow-up information after a meeting, an email is probably the best choice. If you are building a new relationship or discussing sensitive information, in person or a phone call is probably the best approach. Make sure you choose the most appropriate tool for the greatest impact.

9. Give and Receive Feedback
Being able to give and receive respectful and constructive feedback gives us information to refine our skills. It gives us the information we need to move from good to great. Toastmasters International is the perfect example of how feedback can positively impact personal and professional growth. The book, *A Complaint is a Gift* speaks to this concept of how to leverage feedback for success. It's not a failure; it's feedback.

8. Respect
Be courteous and have empathy. When you disagree with someone, it is important for you to be respectful and acknowledge their point of view - EVEN if you don't agree with them. You don't have to agree with somebody to be respectful. Treat others the way you would like them to treat you.

7. Be open minded

Try not to make assumptions or pre-judge a situation. It doesn't cost you anything to have an open mind. A fresh approach can be powerful. This quote by Thomas Dewar sums it up perfectly: *"Minds are like parachutes - they only function when open."*

6. Be confident

Be confident and self-assured in what you are communicating. Establish your expertise and your value. Try not to hesitate. Look people in the eye.

5. Be approachable

Your tone of voice and facial expression directly impacts how people hear you. We all have people in our lives that smile more often than not and those that seem terminally grumpy. Who would you rather talk to?

4. Non-verbal communication

Be aware of your body language. Eye contact, tone of voice, and body posture can have a dramatic effect. I remember my frustration trying to communicate with my pre-teen and the eyeball rolling and big sighs that would always become part of the conversations; not a very effective way to have a productive conversation.

3. Listen

Practice the art of active listening. Listening is harder for some of us than others but necessary. Give your undivided attention, nod encouragement if appropriate and let people finish their thoughts. Don't interrupt unnecessarily. We have all had the experience of speaking with somebody that is always interrupting, and it simply doesn't feel good.

Make sure you give the person you are communicating with your undivided attention. Glancing at your watch, using your smartphone and letting your mind wander are sure signs that you are not listening and giving your full attention.

2. Be clear and concise
Preschool and Kindergarten teachers have this super power. Use descriptive words to paint a visual picture in as simple a way possible. If you are prone to rambling, review your thoughts before you speak and stick to the point. Apply the KISS principle; keep it simple stupid.

1. Know your communication style
Do you understand what your best communication skill is? Do you know where you are the least proficient? Be strategic and use your strengths to get your point across. Leverage what makes you different and what you do best. Understand your communication brand, www.networkconnectsucceed.com/fascinate

These top 10 Communication skills are your "Golden Ticket" to an enriched life filled with mutually satisfying relationships, both personal and business. Use these skills and remember to follow-up and follow through. I encourage you to keep this list handy and view it periodically as a reminder that good communication skills equal success!

"Effective philanthropy requires
a lot of time and creativity
- the same kind of focus and skills
that building a business requires"
~ Bill Gates ~

Practicing Philanthropy as Business

By John Edgcomb

To most, "giving" in the philanthropic sense of giving money is separate from what we do in our business life. We give to charity; we sponsor. We do it for a reason that has a tangible end goal; to help sick kids, veterans, to help save the environment, and the list goes on. For most, including myself, writing checks for these and other causes is cathartic. Let's face it; we feel good when we have extended ourselves to others; be it time or money.

For the purpose of this discussion here, I am talking about philanthropy in business. There seems to be a spiritual dimension to this process, as we put forth good intention for others with no expectation of getting anything back. For many people, the art of making connections and networking only takes us so far. We exchange some business cards, exchange a few humorous antidotes, talk about sports, etc. We never get past the superficial and thus never make a true connection. The meeting has to be about something, your audience. It's about truly listening and asking more questions; what can I do for you? How can I help? And then, making the introduction for that person to another who can add value! This is all about philanthropy because there is, and should be, no expectation of ever getting anything back. If there is, then it's not about your audience, the customer, or your spouse.

This is all easier said than done, and that's the dilemma. And yes, there is the issue of time. Let's step back for a moment and talk about what constitutes the best use of your time. Many people confuse activity with success; when, in actuality, what matters is how meaningful the time you spent was, over the past few hours. Who did you connect with and what was the outcome of that exchange? Did it move you closer to providing value to a customer, friend, or spouse?

Finding the Fortune

I try to meet with someone I don't know, at least one person, every week. In some cases, it's an invite to coffee; in some cases, it is as simple as asking a question or engaging with someone in line at the grocery store, even the cleaners. Opportunities surround us all the time. And, important people that we should know, or could be invaluable in our lives, are often those people we overlook; a neighbor, a friend of a friend and yes, the person standing in line at the grocery store. My business partner was a great example of how this works. A friend had introduced us because they thought we might benefit from each other's expertise…as it turned out, he was right! We started a business together!

You never know; the person you had a conversation with, while in line at the grocery store, may be your new boss's son or daughter. What if….a week later, you met with the son or daughter's father and he happens to be the President of X Company that you are interviewing with? It just so happens that you recognize the kid you talked to last week in the grocery store has the same last name. They even look the same. You say, "Bob, by chance do you have a son going to University of Washington next semester, who is studying to be an architect?" "Why, I do.", he replies. "What a great kid! He is really focused and passionate about designing energy efficient buildings. My brother is an architect who builds energy-efficient homes and office buildings. He may be a good person for your son to talk to about Architecture as a profession. With that kind of introduction, how do you think that interview is going to go? Being aware and understanding your audience is key; but more than that, you made a true and personal connection. The events unfolded in the right way because there was good intention and an openness to take the first step in making the initial connection.

We hear about these kinds of stories all the time. We talk about people being lucky or being in the right place at the right time. I believe they created it, consciously or unconsciously; it happened because the intention was aligned with a lack of expectation. If you go into a meeting with someone with the expectation of getting something out of the meeting, more often than not, there is disappointment. Moreover, by having limited and self-serving expectations, you limit yourself to the possibilities and potential unexpected outcomes of that conversation.

I am working with a young salesman who's in his twenties and sells insurance. It's not an easy job; especially when you have a boss and a large corporate institution setting expectations regarding your sales numbers and monthly quotas. And in many ways, it's not a great way to train a salesperson. Sure, a person needs to establish a pipeline and needs to be accountable for activity, i.e., phone calls and setting up meetings. But the focus should be on how many quality conversations you had today. Do you feel like you helped someone? How? The best sales people sell a brand, themselves as individuals who provide value and not the product.

I was asked to write something to celebrate Jean MacDonald's book, and I can't think of anyone who best exemplifies and lives philanthropically on a daily basis. She connects with everyone and connects people to others in a way that benefits the people she surrounds. Her credibility as a successful businesswoman, her reputation, and her success comes from supporting and adding value to others.

Understanding how philanthropy giving reaches into business, who have you helped lately?

Who could you connect them with?

_____

_____

_____

_____

_____

_____

5

Creativity

In every relationship, the work is never just in the positive actions we do for each other, but in the follow-up.

~ Yehuda Berg ~

The Art of Gratitude and Thank You

Gratitude (noun): the quality of being thankful;
readiness to show appreciation and to return kindness.

Over the past several years I've noticed that we have become a society of busy, multi-tasking, techie people and that somehow the small courtesies of acknowledging kindness, thoughtfulness or extra effort have gotten lost in the shuffle. In my own experience, I have sent gift cards or small holiday gifts to business associates and received no response at all, not even a text or an email. One of those recipients was actually in the business of teaching salespeople about the importance of building extraordinary relationships!

I decided some time ago to do my part to help revive the art of expressing appreciation the old-fashioned way. It's become my mission to personally acknowledge someone every day. I'm sharing my favorite "thank you" technique with you.

It doesn't have to be a Hallmark™
Do you want to make someone feel great and stand out from the competition at the same time? The handwritten note, stamped and sent via snail mail, rules when it comes to generating good feelings and being remembered.

So, your handwriting is awful you say. No worries, there are programs such as OutConnecting.com (my personal white label of OutStand, Inc.) that offer the next best thing; produce your thank you online and they will stamp and mail it for you. It couldn't be easier or more convenient. It will still put you miles ahead of your competitors. A regular part of my daily routine is to send out at least one card a day.

Because I am an author, I often send copies of books to each of my prospects. Of course, each of those books is accompanied by a short, personal note. This makes a lasting impression and is very well received. You can also send birthday cards and notes of congratulation for a promotion or career change. These might also include copies of the articles or press notes where you read the good news.

I use a number of other marketing techniques to promote my business, but none of them outperform the personal note for lasting impact. Every business is looking for the magic bullet, the secret weapon that will set them apart in the marketplace, but most ignore the simplest tool of all, the personal touch. It all comes down to making people feel important.

At a loss for words? Below are a few sample notes. They are simple and to the point:

Dear Bob,

It was a pleasure to have coffee the other day. I'll begin making the introductions we spoke about and hope to reconnect soon. I will give you a call in the next couple of weeks to see how they worked out.

Looking forward to our next meeting,

Jean

Dear Jane,

It's been too long since we last got together. I hope the New Year is going well. I'd like to invite you to the next Toastmasters meeting and will call in the next few days to see if you are available. I'd be pleased to have you attend as my guest.

All the best,

Jean

Dear Jim,

Thank you for your time the other day. As we discussed, we do need to stay in touch. I've made a note on my calendar to follow up in one month.

Talk with you then,

Jean

Dear Pat,

Congratulations on your promotion to Regional Sales Manager! I know you'll be a great success in your new role and wish you all the best. Let's keep in touch.

Sincerely,

Jean

Here's the best way to get started using this powerful follow-up tool: take out your pen, right now and write down the names of the five people you are going to personally thank in the coming week. Then write those notes, send them off, and you've just planted the seeds of five stronger, even more rewarding business relationships.

Escape the Sales Insanity Rut

"The definition of insanity is doing something over and over again and expecting a different result." *Albert Einstein*

These words of wisdom hold especially true for salespeople. If we are not setting ourselves apart from the crowd, not being game changers, we are like the majority of other salespeople out there who simply "wash, rinse, and repeat" when it comes to promoting their products or services.

Are you being creative with your marketing, branding yourself and your product as unique and beneficial to the customer? Or do your email campaigns consist of blasting out a newsletter once a month and waiting for the orders to pour in? Do you know if recipients even open your emails or newsletters? When was the last time you sent out a printed card? Here's another good question to ask yourself: How many notes or emails have you received in the past year thanking you for the great job you've done?

For me, discovering OutConnecting.com has been a game changer. It is the master key I use to unlock responses and grow relationships. It is my self-marketing "buddy." I send out outrageous emails, dynamic newsletters, and beautifully printed cards. Not only do I send them, but I have the tools to determine who opened them and which of those recipients visited my links! This knowledge has become an invaluable resource in my follow-up practices.

I'm bringing this program to your attention because others I have introduced it to have experienced outstanding results:

- An illustrator has increased sales of her work because of the attention-getting email greetings she now sends;

- The mortgage broker who credited the program's enhanced marketing campaigns with the closing of three deals in one week;
- A wedding planner who attributes the personalized marketing (displaying her photo and a beautiful backdrop) with the signing of a big agreement.

You may wonder how easy the program is to use. I like to respond, "Fisher-Price simple." Take the time to learn more today. Escape the sales insanity rut and let's be outrageously creative together! www.OutConnecting.com

What other methods are you using to follow-up and remain connected and engaged with your customers and the marketplace?

**"You have to have confidence
in your ability and then be
tough enough to follow through"**
~ Rosalynn Carter ~

Anatomy of a Script

When you have a "skeleton" of a potential script or an outline, you can absolutely go anywhere!!!!! You'll never be out of words, and you'll never need anyone to write you a script again if you master this line of thinking.

Even the best of those that make appointments have a script in front of them. It doesn't matter if you are calling to: (1) Set up an appointment, (2) Make a customer follow-up call, (3) Schedule a meeting, (4) Invite a guest to an event, (5) Schedule an interview, the sequence is the same!

Enthusiasm: The tone of your voice "Hi John!"

Curiosity: Pique their curiosity with your excitement: "Do you have a few minutes?"

Purpose: "The reason I'm calling you is........

Specific Plan: What are you asking them to do?

WIFM: ("What's in it for me") Tell him/her what is in it for them (benefits to them)

Ask: "Is there any reason why....."

Confirm: Restate what you have agreed on......
Now control your time by asking which is better for you... Tuesday at 3 pm or Thursday at 10 am. Great!

OK, your turn, give it a try! When you know what to say, getting business on your date book is EASY!

Jean MacDonald, DTM • Jean@JeanConnects.com
www.NetworkConnectSucceed.com • Jean MacDonald © 2017 • All Rights Reserved

"Follow your dreams, believe in yourself and don't give up"

~ Rachel Corrie ~

Following Up With Yourself

By Derek Schoch

I learned a long time ago that following up with my customers was critical to business success. One key aspect I had overlooked was the need to follow-up with myself.

That all changed one afternoon when two incidents occurred that altered my business within a matter of hours: my territory was realigned and a top prescribing doctor unexpectedly retired. Those two events threw me for a loop and put me in a tailspin, as I lost over half of my customer base in a single day. I had been in medical device sales for more than ten years. Business was doing well, and I had become comfortable with how things were going. I had never experienced a crisis like this and went into an emotional slump; over and over I kept reliving the drama, asking myself, "Why did this happen to me?" "What did I do to deserve this?" For the next several months, I struggled to get up, get things going again and find a way out of this rut.

One morning I woke up with the realization that I needed to stop blaming circumstances. I decided to follow up on myself and conduct an assessment to figure out how to get back on track. It was time to create some new "checks and balances" for myself.

I began by shifting gears and getting back to the fundamentals, the things I had done when I started in business that helped me to succeed and become top salesperson for my company. This simple change was what it took to reignite my energy and fuel me back toward success. These are the top five components that made the difference:

1 I performed a self-assessment on a weekly/bi-weekly basis.
2. Taking a "birds-eye view" of my territory, I asked myself, "How well do I know the needs of my customers?"
3. I practiced Learn-to-Earn, by doing further research on my product, company, and competitors.
4. I became focused on strong and persistent follow-up (being efficient at daily job tasks, handwritten thank you notes, making phone calls, etc).
5. Most importantly, I developed a strong and positive mental attitude.

Today, by using these valuable tools, my territory is back at the top. Being proactive with yourself, you should conduct an honest "check up from the neck up," take ownership of your attitude and make today a little better than yesterday.

The Three Ring Circus

Mastering the art of the trade expo

Ladies and gentlemen, let me introduce you to what I call the Three Ring Circus:

- **In the first ring,** we have rows and rows of expo or trade show booths, with people sitting behind each table, most chatting with co-workers, some setting up banners or graphic displays, maybe even a rotating wheel or game of chance. The basic strategy is to lure prospects in with giveaway trinkets, get them to stay and spin the wheel or roll the dice and then linger to check out the goods or services. The "midway" is finally lit up and ready for the gates to open, but are we prepared to deliver the goods?

- **In the second ring** are the breakout sessions, workshops, and demonstrations that the audience can choose to attend. The program handouts make each one sound so tempting that it's hard for attendees to select from what's being offered.

- **In the third ring** is the midway traffic itself, all the attendees wandering up and down the many aisles. They will either stop at our booth or pass us by. Of the ones who do stop, many are simply window shoppers, trick-or-treating to fill their handy goodie bags with the free stuff, but not staying long enough to learn more about us. Sound familiar? We've all done it ourselves.

I have attended and presented at many of these events over the years. When I started out in the insurance business, the standard setup was a plain, vanilla booth with stacks of brochures on the table. One or two of my colleagues and I would stand behind the table dressed in our business suits and hope to catch the eye and interest of someone from the stream of traffic that passed by.

"Step right up, folks, you don't wanna miss this!"

Thank goodness I learned about being creative when I moved into the cosmetics business. That's where I acquired the skills and techniques to make myself, my product and my brand stand out from the rest of the midway sideshows. At one event, a huge product expo, we purchased a double booth and parked my pink Cadillac in the space. We filled it with pink balloons and surrounded it with bowls of pink heart candy and lipstick sample giveaways. We maximized our time, money and effort by rotating staff in shifts from our 10-person sales team to ensure we were always fresh and ready to engage with every visitor to our booth.

Because of the pre-event strategies we had developed, we acquired many new leads and prospects at this competitive event. As the leader of our team, I took responsibility for making sure we did all the right things to leverage our investment in being part of the show. Here are a few of the ways we corralled leads and made great connections:

- Though this was a number of years ago before cell phones were common and tabletop computer sign-up stations were available to capture follow-up information, we got the job done by creating simple paper registration forms that doubled as contest entries to guess the number of balloons in our pink Cadillac.

- We had thank you cards with us which were already prepared with stamps on envelopes and were ready to mail immediately to each of our new contacts along with a brief, handwritten note to the attendee.

- We made notes on the back of every business card or completed registration form, noting who had met with the attendee and the level of interest in either our products or the possibility of becoming a consultant with us.

- We had visited every single vendor before the show opened, handing out our pink goodie bags until it seemed there was a sea of pink bags in the expo center. We also made sure we took bags to the different people manning the booths at various times of the day, and we never overlooked the men. We knew they would take the bags home to their wives or girlfriends, drawing even more prospects. Men were actually some of our best customers and also referred a number of new consultants to our team.

- We planned in advance to have team members in attendance at each of the breakout sessions, always with our name tags on, business cards in hand and big smiles on our faces.

Our preparation and enthusiasm made us a standout hit at this major event. Each of us also brought an extra pair of shoes to change into, sparing our feet and ensuring we were still smiling at the end of the day. Below is a recap of my top seven tips to help you have a successful expo experience, every time:

1. **Dress for success.** Looking professional, friendly and approachable is the goal.
2. **Be creative and make your booth as attractive as possible.** Solicit input, ideas and setup help from all members of your Expo team.
3. **Get out from behind the table!** Meet the traffic in the aisles as they approach. Invite and welcome them to your booth.
4. **Be enthusiastic, caring and sharing.** Approach every contact with the attitude of helping them by providing the product or service solution they've been looking for.
5. **Plan ahead and have plenty of supplies on hand,** this includes brochures, business cards, giveaways, forms and follow-up cards. Make sure everything is labeled with your contact information.
6. **Have those follow up cards ready to go.** It is extremely important that you get them in the hands of each contact within three days of the event while "the sizzle" is still there and you still have their attention.

7. **Now follow-up by making your calls!** You already have
   a warm lead in your hands; and that alone makes it well
   worth the effort to pick up the phone and continue building
   that relationship. Review your contact notes before you
   call, then set up an appointment or coffee conversation to
   keep the dialogue going.

So many exhibitors sabotage themselves and become victims
of "vendors' remorse," wondering why no one stopped at their
booths, blaming poor traffic and complaining that all anyone
wanted was the candy. Instead, make your experience one of the
success stories. With some pre-planning on your part, a positive
and enthusiastic attitude, an inviting display, and timely follow up,
you and your business can be among the standout, memorable
vendors at any event. These are great opportunities to mine
the gold that comes streaming through the doors in the form of
prospects who are seeking solutions you can provide.

Think of yourself as the ringmaster of this three ring circus.

Generating excitement, introducing your products or services, shining the spotlight on the benefits and value they provide and welcoming a whole new audience of customers and prospects.

What are you doing to prepare for your next trade show?

"Take a bite"

6

PRODUCTIVITY

2% Impact
2% Inspiration
96% Time & Repetition

"Change will not come if we wait for some other person or some other time. We are the ones we've been waiting for. We are the change that we seek."

~ Barack Obama ~

When is Enough Enough?

Full speed ahead or not? Are you ready to move on to the next challenge? Are you mad enough, sad enough, tough enough, tired enough, fed up enough to get out of the rut that you're stuck in?

The ideas seem to flow from everywhere. Do this to succeed, try that to move forward, take this path or that one to get to your next goal. What all these internal messages are really saying is that you need to make a change, except that you're not ready to take that step. You try making one more powerful New Year's resolution to get yourself jump-started, but then you run out of steam, become frustrated and quit. Sound familiar?

When is enough enough?

The truth is, we will only make a change when we understand what we need to do, develop a strategy to do it, and become vested in the process. We'll change only when we're ready and not a minute sooner.

A good example was my quest to earn the Pink Cadillac with Mary Kay Cosmetics. As a sales director, my team and I were earning Grand Ams but making that leap to creating a plan and doing the work needed to see that Cadillac appear in my driveway just wasn't happening.

I got my reality check when one day my husband said to me, "Why do you keep telling everyone you're going to earn that Pink Caddy? It's becoming embarrassing." He followed that up by asking, "What is it that you need to do to meet the sales goal?"

This was at the end of November, and I told him that to earn that car I had to finish out the year with an additional $23,000 in sales.

If that didn't happen, the slate was wiped clean and I started all over again on January 1st. "Have you ever done $23,000 in one month?" he asked. "No," I muttered. The kicker came when he said, "Then what makes you think you can?"

Sometimes motivation comes wrapped in optimism and a burst of energy – other times it's fueled by a slow burn. His challenging remark made me so angry that it lit the fire that motivated me to make a strategy, pursue the goal and together with my team, we earned the first of several pink Cadillacs!

It was the decision to map out a plan, to persevere and take the action needed that got the job done. Those were the changes that I had to make to earn the prize. Enough was enough!

Ideas and ingenuity are great resources for setting goals, but until we are ready to make essential changes ourselves, our situation doesn't change at all.

When is enough enough?

Is it time to make a change?
Put down your thoughts.

_____

_____

_____

_____

_____

_____

_____

_____

_____

_____

_____

_____

_____

_____

_____

_____

_____

_____

_____

_____

_____

_____

_____

_____

**"Before anything else,
preparation is the key to success."**
~ Alexander Graham Bell ~

How Prepared Are You?

**"One important key to success is self-confidence.
An important key to self confidence is preparation."**
~ Arthur Ashe ~

Do you feel as though you're constantly playing catch-up, barely staying on top of all the tasks you want to accomplish in your business and personal life? If that's your reality, it's time to ask yourself these questions: What does your upcoming week or month look like? Do you have a plan, a strategy to designate the time you need to get the work done? Or do you "play it by ear," changing your schedule on the fly, trying to keep up?

Let me offer some insights that may help. The concept has been tailored by others. Though my weeks are never the same, I set aside time to plan them out in advance. I categorize my meetings, tasks, and goals into three main categories I can visualize:

Productive days: These are the days I designate to move my business forward, seeing prospects, clients, making new appointments, calling or sending notes to decision makers and following up on warm leads. I also attend networking events, followed by those invaluable "coffee conversations" (see Chapter 6).

Creative days: These days are generally spent in the office, and I call them "butt-in-the-seat time." They are the days I follow up with the people I have met or had coffee with, work on project-related tasks, make research calls and read to keep up on topics relevant to my clients and business. This is also my writing time, spent generating newsletters and managing my blog and social media activity.

Play days: These days are spent completely free of business activities. No emails, no computer, no phone calls, no work, period. This is time I spend focused on myself or activities with my family.

By developing a system that addresses your priorities in life and then making it a habit to do the advance planning, you are able to reduce stress, be far more productive and enjoy the benefit of more free time. It's also easier to be diligent about digging into tasks on the days they need to be done when you know that working the plan reaps those rewards down the line.

The following page offers a weekly and monthly planning template that you can use to develop a strategy tailored to your specific needs. Establish a monthly monetary goal and use it to help define the weekly priorities that are the foundation of a successful plan. One card, one email and one meeting set with a decision maker each working day should head the list. Networking and "being seen" in your marketplace should follow. Newsletters, blogging and social media activity that keep you and your business connected with clients, colleagues, referrers, and new prospects complete the list of weekly priorities.

Once you've established the habit of weekly planning, integrate the weeks and months into a quarterly format. This will enable you to see the "big picture" and also allow for activities which need more preparation. Advance planning of play days, extended training, away seminars and vacations can be a powerful incentive to staying focused and productive in the long term. It also ensures that you build in tasks and goals before and after those periods, so your calendar isn't empty when you return resulting in the need to chase business rather than catching it.

Having a system that you will actually use and adapt to your needs is important to maximizing your success. It may be challenging to stick with it at first, but once you make a habit of using a solid, fundamental planning system it becomes a dynamic, moving part of your business. One that you fine tune and adjust as needed to keep you from being overwhelmed on the road to reaching your goals. It is an essential element to both making connections and to managing that all important aspect of your business: following through and following up.

Another tool that has been added to my toolbox of planning is *Best Self Journal*. Learn more at networkconnectsucceed.com/sales-tools.

Plan Your Week: Manage Your Time

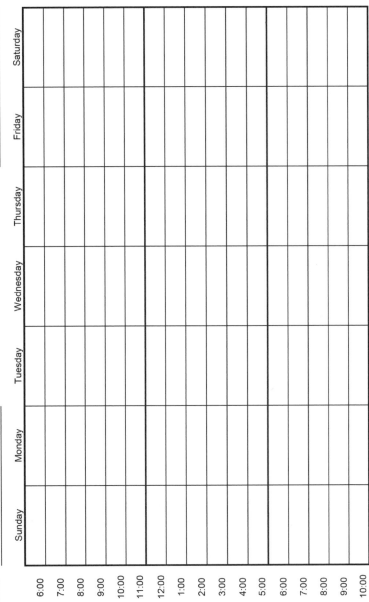

Name: _____

Week of: _____

	Sunday	Monday	Tuesday	Wednesday	Thursday	Friday	Saturday
6:00							
7:00							
8:00							
9:00							
10:00							
11:00							
12:00							
1:00							
2:00							
3:00							
4:00							
5:00							
6:00							
7:00							
8:00							
9:00							
10:00							

Jean MacDonald, DTM • Jean@JeanConnects.com
www.NetworkConnectSucceed.com/resources
Jean MacDonald © 2017 • All Rights Reserved

Finding the Fortune

MONTHLY GOAL PLANNER   Month _____

Tracking Results

	Week1	Week 2	Week 3	Week 4	Week 5	Total
Weekly Contact Goal						
Contacts *What do want I to achieve?*						
Weekly Monetary Goal						
Monetary Goal *What do I want to achieve?*						
Prospecting Summary						
Networking Meetings						
Text / Emails						
Phone Calls						
Organization / Contact Manager						
Lunches/Coffees Face-to-Face						
Social Media Posts						
Continued Follow-Up Notes / Calls / Emails						
Leads Generated						
Monthly Recap						

Achievements   Challenges

Follow up is the key to it all!

97% make 1-2 attempts
67% make 3-4 attempts
23% make 5-7 attempts

48% never follow up
25% make a second attempt
12% make 3 attempts and stop

The Kicker
80% of the sales are made
in the 5-12 attempt!

Life Lessons Ring True

It's interesting how many of the life lessons I learned in my childhood I apply in business today. Interesting, but not surprising. Those childhood experiences taught me to treat others with courtesy, sincerity, and respect; traits as important to conducting business as an adult as they were to "growing up right." Some of the lessons I remember best were about communicating with others on the phone.

I was about twelve when I assumed true telephone responsibilities in our household. During the Vietnam era, my father served as an airlift commander for the Air Force. He was responsible for the logistics of shipping troops and equipment around the world. He was often on call and needed to be reachable day or night. One of my proudest moments came when dad sat me down and taught me how to handle the important calls that would be coming in; I felt so grown up and was delighted to think of myself as his special assistant. We sat at the kitchen table and role-played until I felt comfortable responding to calls and taking messages. Then came the lesson in follow-up: getting the time right, the caller's name, number and other specifics, and alerting my father wherever he might be. I quickly lost any nervousness I may have had and came to enjoy a feeling of accomplishment each time I connected with a caller.

For many business people, connecting via phone has fallen out of favor over the past several years, replaced by text messaging and emailing. Taking time to engage on the phone is frequently seen as a time-waster; why do it when you can click a few keys to get the message across or the task done? In many situations, texting and emailing are the practical and efficient choices. But, has your smartphone outsmarted you? Are you opting for the quick and easy functions it offers, and missing the bigger dollars and stronger relationships a personal connection could be bringing you? Have you started to avoid using the phone, seeing it as a time robber rather than a valuable resource in your business toolkit? These are symptoms of a bad case of phone phobia.

Take some time this coming week to connect the old-fashioned way. While efficiency is highly prized by salespeople and customers alike, there are some situations when hearing a person's voice over the phone brings added depth to a business transaction, strengthening the relationship and opening the door to new possibilities. Cure phone phobia by thinking of the time spent as an investment with potentially high returns and be diligent in following up on those new opportunities.

The next page offers my list of five handy tips for beating phone phobia and building your connection and follow-up skills.

Five Tips for Beating Phone Phobia

1. **Make your calls with a purpose in mind.** Are you calling to make the first contact with someone, is this a follow-up call to provide information, or are you trying to close a deal? Identify the types of calls you make most often and then create a simple script for each of them. What will your opening statement be? What are the talking points you need to cover? Practice the script until the words flow naturally and you are comfortable adapting it as needed. Best advice by far: role play the calls with a friend or colleague. It's a great way to practice overcoming objections and raise your confidence sky high!

2. **Know your products or services well.** Be knowledgeable and familiar with the value and benefits of what you are selling. Stay in the loop about enhancements or upgrades that make those products or services stand out from the competition. If you don't know the answer to a question, rather than wing it, tell the customer that you'll check on that and call them back. Be credible and as always *– follow through and follow-up!*

3. **Make "How can I help you?" the core of each call.** Read it, feel it, believe it. Approach each phone connection with that goal in mind and watch your numbers soar. All human beings, especially customers, want to feel important and to know that you have their best interests at heart. When you are sincere, they will pick up on that and be much more willing to listen to what you have to offer.

4. **Think of "No" as a new opportunity.** The fear of rejection is probably the biggest deterrent to initiating successful phone contacts, but it doesn't have to be. When a prospect says "No," a door hasn't slammed a new one has opened. You now have the opportunity to ask additional questions, identify objections and then build value rather than doing a hard sell. The best salespeople in the world think of "No" as an incentive to learn more about the needs of their customers and in the process, build even stronger relationships.

5. **Timing is everything.** Make calls when you are feeling your best. We all have peak periods of the day when we are better at doing some tasks than others. Figure out when your "phone call window" is and then just do it – make those calls! Don't assume the other person is too busy, may not be available, or might be at lunch. If you find yourself making those kinds of excuses, an accountability partner will help you stay on track, and productive phone connections will become another key to your success!

For additional resources visit www.NetworkConnectSucceed.com/resources

7

Persistence

**Patience, persistence
and perspiration
make an unbeatable
combination for success.**
~ Napoleon Hill ~

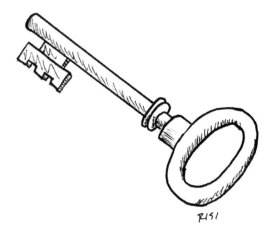

RISI

Following Up is Key

You can find connections everywhere, even where you least expect them. Early one morning, I stopped at the local Dunkin' Donuts for some coffee. Though the line of customers stretched out the door, I decided it was worth the wait to get my caffeine fix. As I took my place at the end of the line, the woman in front of me turned and commented, "With this kind of traffic, I should own one of these stores."

I laughed and told her I didn't think I'd enjoy getting up a the crack of dawn to make donuts. I was glad I already had a business of my own. Curious, she asked what I did, and I explained that I helped women to feel good by showing them how to look their best with Mary Kay cosmetics and that the company offered wonderful opportunities.

Her eyes lit up, and she told me that she was a Girl Scout troop leader, and had been looking for someone to come and talk with the girls about skin care. I was interested in helping and took her information, promising to be in touch.

A woman in line behind us had overheard our conversation and inquired about Mary Kay hand treatment products. She was a nurse and asked if I would consider coming to the medical facility where she worked to provide some pampering for the nurses there. I gladly took her contact information and assured her she would be hearing from me.

The connection vibration was still going strong as a man who was standing behind the nurse then asked if I'd be able to speak with his sister. He told me she loved Mary Kay products but had recently lost her longtime representative. Naturally, I promised to contact her as well.

Three strong leads, simply from chatting with people in line and all before 7:30 a.m.

The opportunities had presented themselves, and now I needed to take action to realize the true potential of these connections. At this point, all I had were leads. Sure, they were strong leads, but they would mean nothing unless I followed up on each of them. Following up is the key to sales and team building; the key that turned these connections into success stories:

- I arranged with the Girl Scout leader to share skin care tips and a pampering session with twelve girls and several of their mothers. The troop leader was so impressed with the experience and the products that she became a new consultant on my team.

- The nurse was also so pleased with the products and information I shared at her office that she asked for an individual session and became a new consultant as well.

- The third connection, the sister of the man I spoke with in line, was the icing on the cake. It turned out that she was a local mortician and liked Mary Kay products so much because they gave luster and life to the skin of her "customers." She ultimately referred me to several other area funeral homes, resulting in nearly $3,000 in product sales!

The benefits of these initial connections expanded like ripples on a pond. My team became supporters of the community through ongoing sessions with the Girl Scouts, we developed a strong referral business with area nurses, medical practices, and funeral directors and we went on to earn our first Pink Cadillac.

Making connections is one of the most exciting and rewarding aspects of building relationships and generating sales. Timely, effective follow-up is critical to achieving those goals. The ultimate benefit of networking extends far beyond meeting people. Following up and following through ensures that you will continue to connect and reconnect, over and over again.

Follow up and follow through are key to building a strong, successful business.

What is the key follow-up event that has ensured continued connections? Think about it and do it again.

_____

_____

_____

_____

_____

_____

_____

_____

_____

_____

_____

_____

_____

_____

_____

_____

_____

_____

_____

_____

_____

_____

_____

Ambition is the path to success, persistence is the vehicle you arrive in.

~ William Eardley, IV ~

Follow-Up Helps a Holiday Deal Pay Off

by Sara Velander

I had been a financial representative for about a year when I attended my first agency Christmas party. One of my colleagues had obviously been enjoying the "Christmas cheer" and was loudly complaining that he had so much work to do that he couldn't keep his head on straight and didn't even have time to call on new leads. Impulsively I blurted out, "I'll take them off your hands!" Imagine my surprise when he agreed. He told me he would buy the leads, I would do the work, and we'd share the business. He had money and no time, and as a young representative, I had time but no money. I considered it to be my lucky day, even if a liberal amount of alcohol had helped to seal the deal.

At first, I was terrible. My "partner" bought the leads, and I diligently made the calls. When he asked me how things were going, I had nothing to show for it. No one was scheduling appointments with me, and my frustration level was rising daily.

Then one morning, after some more dead end calls, I remembered an experience I had as a young Girl Scout. It was time for our annual fundraiser which that meant I needed to sell some cookies. Excited about my first chance to participate, I sat on a stool next to our phone, calling everyone on my mother's list of neighbors' phone numbers. I didn't know who half the people were, but they all knew my family and patiently entertained the call of an 8-year old Brownie talking excitedly about thin mints and peanut butter patties.

As I reflected back on that memory, I realized that I needed to make that same kind of connection with the people I was calling now. I sat down at the phone and started making calls, using my voice to express the same level of enthusiasm for our services as that young Girl Scout had used to sell cookies. You know what?

People started scheduling appointments with me! Suddenly I was on fire and scheduling lots of appointments. People starting buying and business really took off! The end result: my partner and I made All-American that year, top 100 in sales for the company and earned a trip to Hawaii as a reward.

Even better, many of those leads and sales have turned into long-term relationships. One woman attended my baby shower, and when I opened my new office, her husband gave me furniture at no cost. Another plays golf with me at an annual tournament. I still receive holiday cards from many of those clients as well. Learning to make quality connections has been rewarding in many ways. The bottom line is that all these relationships were a result of following up and following through on an opportunity that I happened to walk into at a company Christmas party.

Traveling on the Road to Success

By Phil Gafka

Sometimes fortune smiles down on you and you are the beneficiary of a life lesson that truly carries impact through the course of your life. Such is one of my first lessons in the Success of Following Up.

My first job out of college was a traveling salesperson for a product manufacturer. Here's your territory, here are your product brochures, now go forth and sell. My travels took me throughout Wisconsin, "America's Dairyland," truly the heartland of our country.

I began by making a first lap around my new territory, targeting potential customers and hoping to build a successful customer base. Part of the challenge was figuring out how to efficiently travel around the large state and use my time well. Typically, I made a first call on a prospective customer, introduced myself and my wares and was given a polite amount of time to assure the prospect that we were a reputable vendor and would take good care of his business needs. The calls usually ended with a courteous "Thanks for the information", and then I was sent on my way.

On my next lap around Wisconsin I made my second sales calls and followed up with the prospects. Again, I was given a polite amount of time to state my case and provide any additional information about the benefits our great product could offer the prospect. Again, most of them would smile, nod, and send me on my way.

One morning I began my third rotation through the territory, stopping in for yet another prospect call. This one was different, however. Before I could begin my regular spiel, the prospect began the meeting himself. He welcomed me back and told me that before we went any further, he had something for me. With that said he lifted up his desk blotter and removed a completed purchase order. Not a large order, but an order nonetheless. With a smile, he handed it to me and told me they were looking forward to doing business with me and my company.

Surprised and pleased, I thanked him, and as I read over the order, I noticed that the date typed on it was that of my last call to his business. My new customer went on to explain that many salespeople came into his office, sat across the desk from him and promised the moon and the stars, only never to be heard from again. Occasionally a salesperson might return for a second call, but after that would disappear as well.

What he had discovered over the years was that the salesperson who persisted and followed up enough to make a third call almost invariably represented the type of vendor they wanted to do business with. That became his personal benchmark for doing business so much so that his standard practice was to prepare a purchase order after the second call. In the rare event of that third visit he would place an order, knowing that the salesperson was as serious about doing business as he was.

As I look back, I realize that all those road trips were well worth my time and efforts because they taught me that persistence and follow-up are the first steps on the road to business success.

The Coffee Conversation: Quest for Opportunities

"Imagine there is a sign around everyone's neck that says, 'Make me feel important!'"
Mary Kay Ash, founder of Mary Kay Cosmetics

You'll hear me mention the coffee conversation over and over again, those informal "getting to know you" meetings you have at the local coffee shop or café after connecting with someone while networking or calling on prospects. Don't take them lightly; these seemingly casual chats can also be one of the most powerful keys to your success. Why? Because they take place in a relaxed, friendly setting, perfect for asking questions and learning more about the other person's needs. Learning more is essential to identifying new opportunities.

The heart of your business lies in the ability to ask the right questions. Take some time to think about what you hope to learn from most of the people you talk with; asking questions without a goal in mind might result in a great cup of coffee but little else. There is certain information you'll want to learn about virtually everyone you meet with: where are they doing business and who are they working with now? What kind of challenges have they been facing, and how can you help them?

It's also important to phrase your questions in a positive way, especially when meeting with power partners or seasoned businesspeople. Don't let the conversation drift into a gripe session about the state of the economy, employee turnover, or yet another new tax; instead, focus on questions geared toward finding creative solutions to specific challenges they may be facing. In my last book, *Get Up, Get Dressed and Get Out the Door,* I provided a list of helpful business interview questions. I have updated and adapted that list on the following pages, to assist you in making the most of your coffee conversations.

A few years ago, I met with a wedding planner, and we had a great conversation that resulted in a client for me. We met again a month later. She was very pleased that I had a bride to send her way. I followed up by calling her again in a couple of months, and we met the next week. As we chatted, I happened to ask her what her husband did. She told me he was a global director for a major food and beverage company in the Chicago area. I was thrilled to learn this as I had wanted to do business with this company for some time but had no connections to pave the way with a referral. She told me she would talk with her husband. He and I spoke within the week. This led to a personal introduction to the president of the corporation's Women's Leadership team, and we were off and running. I was invited to present about my business and then hired to come in and work with her team.

Not every conversation will result in a sale or new client. You may both discover that, while it's enjoyable chatting, you don't have much in common in terms of doing business. I enjoy knowing more about the people I meet: what do they like about the community, how many children do they have, where is their spouse or partner employed? It's another way to build good connections. Who knows where things might lead down the road. Regardless of the meeting outcome, I still send a follow-up email or personal note, thanking my new contact for his or her time.

Never underestimate the power of a coffee conversation! By asking the right questions and practicing good follow-up, each meeting has the potential to help take your business to the next level of success.

"Meeting once is nice, twice is great, building relationships is priceless!" - *Jean*

The key to networking is showing up and being memorable

The Quest for Opportunities:
Business Building Coffee Conversation

Creating Connections
1. Tell me a little bit about yourself.
2. What do you enjoy most about what you do?
3. Where do you see yourself in the next 5 years?
4. Let's discuss things we may have in common.

Developing Relationships
1. What is your biggest challenge?
2. How can I help you grow your business?
3. Who can I introduce you to?
4. Let me tell you about the organizations I am involved in.
5. Who do you know you could introduce me to?

For additional resources visit www.NetworkConnectSucceed.com/resources

LADDER OF CREDIBILITY

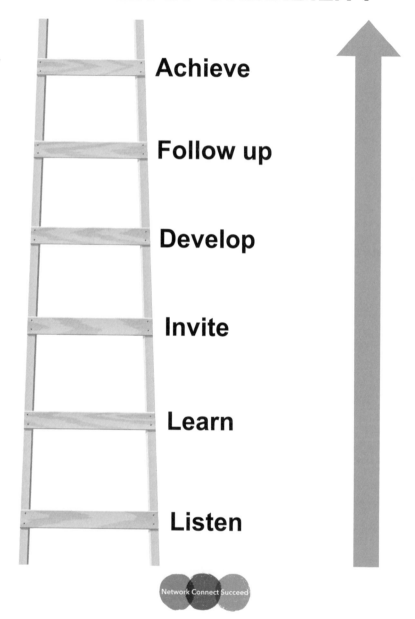

Achieve

Follow up

Develop

Invite

Learn

Listen

Network Connect Succeed

For additional resources visit www.NetworkConnectSucceed.com

**Success is not final, failure is
not fatal; it is the courage
to continue that counts.**
~ Winston Churchill ~

**Knowledge is key
but it is the
perseverance that
gets it done!**
~ Jean MacDonald ~

Conclusion

Just a follow-up at the end...

My mantra is "Meeting once is nice, twice is great, building relationships is priceless." Several people have asked me, "How have you had so much success?" My answer is simple, "5,467 cups of coffee." Yes, over all these years it was meeting people, and it was following up!

I encourage you to meet with your contacts more than once. Don't reach out once and give up if you had a synergy. Not everyone is going to be the right fit, but without getting to know them, you will never know.

As I commented in the introduction, follow-up is simple but not always easy. Our lives are filled with stuff. Our email is fuller than ever and finding time for anything today sometimes seems impossible.

But, imagine if you were to make a vow to yourself to reach out to just one new person a day. Invite them for the cup of coffee (See tips for Business Building Coffee Conversation in Chapter 7). Ask them questions and see what you have in common. By asking the right questions and taking good notes on what you learn, you'll find clues to help them, and in turn, they could help you. Think of all the connections you could make! Have you ever heard of the idea of the "six degrees of separation"? As the world gets smaller, our social network gets larger. I guarantee you will be surprised to find out just who knows who!

It definitely takes time and effort to build your network. Plan your week (see the weekly planner and Monthly Goal Planner in Chapter 6). Have fun and be in the moment with people. Be strategic with your time. Write the personal notes and bring a smile to someone's face every day. You have to be "Interested to be Interesting."

I would like to thank you for taking the time to read this book. My hope is that you will find at least one action that will help you develop your social network into the business of your dreams.

The fortune is truly sitting right in front of us...

Remember to follow-up, follow your heart, and follow through with your promises.

All my best,

Contributors

John Edgcomb
Cutting Edge Connect, Inc.
www.ceconnectinc.com
john@ceconnectinc.com
847-856-9643

Cutting edge Connect was created by top-performing recruiters and business executives from Fortune 500 companies with one objective: Improve the hiring process for decision makers and hiring authorities. It is our mission to build our client companies one qualified hire at a time, bringing together talented people and engaged employers for the purpose of filling openings and reducing turnover. Our efforts have cut hiring time and drastically reduced fulfillment costs for dozens of worldwide leaders in manufacturing, print production, engineering, and healthcare. We work with organizations on three separate continents and have placed talent at all levels for our client companies.

Phil Gafka, CBC
LEAP Associates, Inc.
www.leapassociates.com
phil@leapassociates.us
847-212-4903

Phil is a seasoned executive, and now as a Certified Business Coach, he draws on his successful experience to help individuals, teams, and organizations to develop and grow their leadership skills, healthy cultures, and results-oriented strategies.

Contributors

Andy Horner
Outstand, Inc.
www.outstand.com
andyhorner@outstand.com
800-865-7496

Andy, CEO at Outstand, is the inventor, product manager and creative force behind outstand.com, the online communication platform the helps business people accelerate relationships. Through software, webinars, speaking and consulting, Andy helps salespeople and entrepreneurs differentiate themselves, activate their creativity and become outstanding.

Lynn Lionhood
LegalShield
www.legalshield.com/hub/lynnrlionhood
RHL6807@gmail.com
630-697-6889

I provide assistance to businesses and employee groups with their employee benefits as well as providing strategic consulting with small businesses. We also provide plans for individuals to assist in legal and identity theft/restoration services.

Leslie Lipps
Your Marketing Department
www.leslielipps.com
leslie@leslielipps.com
847-223-2692

Market Strategy & Brand Specialist. Leslie offers cutting edge ideas and strategies to develop or refresh your brand. She communicates in a visually engaging way to offer high- quality deliverables. She has been in the creative services and marketing industry for over 28 years and enjoys all of the different roles and services that work together to create effective branding.

Contributors

Dobie Maxwell
Uranus Unlimited Inc.
www.dobiemaxwell.com
dobiemaxwell@aol.com

Dobie Maxwell has been a nationally touring standup comedy headliner for years. He also teaches classes for aspiring comedians and speakers in addition to punching up speech copy for corporate clients.

Jim Mecir
ImprovTalk
jimmecir@improvtalk.com
www.improvtalk.com
847-922-5486

As a former Major League Baseball Pitcher, who was born with a club foot, Jim Mecir is well adept to overcoming adversity to realize his dreams and achieve success. As an engaging keynote speaker for ImprovTalk with his partner, Ellen Schnur, a Second City trained improviser, the two teach improvisation skills to solve everyday workplace challenges, build successful teams, improve communication and persevere through challenging times. To learn more about Jim visit: jimmecir.com. Jim can be reached at jimmecir@gmail.com.

Contributors

Howard Prager

Advance Learning Group
www.advancelearninggroup.com
howard@advancelearninggroup.com
224-595-6432

Advance Learning Group focuses on learning and reinventing leadership development, working with organizations, non-profits, and government agencies. Through attention to detail and keen listening, we learn about your needs and translate them to action through consultation, instructional design, facilitation, measurement, and coaching.

Having won 8 awards for professional excellence prior to starting Advance Learning Group, Howard Prager ensures achieving and exceeding your desired results is what matters most whether facilitating a board retreat or collaborating on new initiatives.

Aaron Risi

Yo Arty! Illustrations
www.yoarty.com
aaronrisi@yahoo.com
410-746-7845

An award winning, out of the box artist and published cartoonist. Looking for that special art that will set you apart? Aaron is a classically trained artist, influenced by surrealism. His work is created with a bold, energizing style. He has developed art for authors, musicians, and nonprofit organizations.

Contributors

Ellen Schnur
Improv Talk
www.improvtalk.com
ellen.schnur@improvtalk.com
847-987-6158

"Yes, And" your way to innovation and stronger connections with Improv Talk's highly interactive workshops. You will discover direct applications to your work and life, bringing back strategies you can implement immediately!

Derek Schoch
www.networkconnectsucceed.com/dschoch
derekschoch@yahoo.com
443-802-2953

Derek is an experienced goal-driven sales professional with more than eighteen years in B2B, retail and medical sales. Being a thought-leader, coach and speaker, Derek uses his creative talents teaching sales development, communication branding and business strategy.

Zachary Slade
GCG Financial, LLC
GCGFinancial.com
Zcslade@gmail.com
C: 224-257-5011

Zach works in the Risk Management division of GCG Financial, LLC. He prides himself on his unique ability to help mid-sized companies simplify and understand their risk management and commercial insurance needs. Zach resides in Lake Bluff, IL and volunteers as the Vice President of Fresh Start Business Incubator a 501(c)(3) non-for-profit organization.

Contributors

Eddie Soto
E.S. Online Enterprises, Inc.
www.ESOnlineBiz.com
eddie@esonlinebiz.com

Custom websites, Social Media suites, Wordpress sites, Newsletters, Blogs and SEO for small business. Certified SBA/ SBDC advisor. Helping businesses create a clearer, more defined online presence through multi-channel marketing tools. Speaker, Trainer, Presenter, Social Media Training Programs.

Sara Velander
COUNTRY Financial®
www.countryfinancial.com/sara.velander
sara.velander@countryfinancial.com
847-548-2120

Sara Velander is a Financial Representative at COUNTRY Financial, who has been in and around the financial industry her whole life. She helps her clients understand how all of the financial pieces of their lives intersect – from home insurance, to business planning, to protecting income, to planning for their children's education, to retirement, and through each stage of their long-term financial security.

Acknowledgements

It takes an extraordinary team to make this dream come true. I am so fortunate to have surrounded myself with smart, caring individuals that share the vision.

Leslie Lipps, my marketing and brand specialist, with her diligence, kept the ball rolling. She is so creative, and I love her out of the box thinking. She always says, "Let's get it done. I am here for you."

Christine Schaefer, my editor/writer, was the newest addition to our team. How much fun it is to work with Chris. Her insight and research were the icing on the cake.

Aaron Risi, who shared his cartooning talent. Wow! Son, you have come a long way. This is just the beginning, get your pencil ready for the next book. Your ideas and fun drawings made the book come alive.

Thank you to all those who shared their stories and experiences.

To all my family, thank you for your support and insight. Greg, my husband who cheers me on, I love you so much. I appreciate your encouragement and patience.

For those that I have not named individually, I am sincerely grateful for your friendship and insight.

About the Author

Jean MacDonald creates a spark of inspiration wherever she presents. Combining enthusiasm with an energetic speaking style, she conveys her messages with the power, passion, and presence proven to motivate others to achieve their goals and dreams.

Jean knows that attitude is 95 percent of the winning score, and this is reflected in how she relates to her audience and inspires them to be the best they can be. Jean is a dedicated leader – motivating, educating and empowering – yet a woman who speaks from the heart with a touch of humility. Having risen through the ranks in the challenging commercial insurance industry while raising and supporting three children single-handedly, Jean openly shares her life lessons with others. Jean was a leader in the commercial insurance industry where she grew a small business into a multi-million dollar revenue producer.

She would later take that same brand of leadership and success to the well-known Mary Kay Cosmetics Company where her extraordinarily high sales volume and leadership, earned her the use of the company's signature cars twelve times, five being their trophy "Pink Cadillac." Jean was not only a top producer; she but was also a top recruiter and trainer of her Mary Kay teams nationwide.

As an author and compassionate humanitarian, Jean donates a portion of the proceeds from her books to helping people in job transitions through the non-profit, Fresh Starts. *"Get Up, Get Dressed, and Get Out The Door!"*- published in 2012, received rave reviews.

More recently, Jean has parlayed her highly successful networking, leadership and sales skills into an exciting corporate training-centric business. Jean designs tailored programs that help guide individuals and businesses on how to "connect the dots" to strong, reliable relationships through the development and implementation of robust business outreach and training strategies. With the use of proprietary marketing tools, Jean awakens the potential in leaders and sales teams. She adds excitement to a company's employee morale and creates a strategically tailored blueprint for creating an energized, focused, workforce that works together to enhance a company's overall growth and success.

Jean is an admired public speaker, earning the Distinguished Toastmasters designation and is also part of the National Speaker's Association. Her compelling, often humorous stories have empowered thousands of people in cities throughout the country helping individuals, teams and businesses to realize their maximum sales potential.

Originally from New Jersey, Jean now lives in North Carolina with her husband, Greg. She is the proud mother of three children and a loving grandmother to three beautiful girls.

BOOK JEAN MACDONALD
TO SPEAK AT YOUR
NEXT EVENT

When it comes to choosing a professional speaker, Jean delivers. By sharing her compelling and often humorous stories, she has empowered thousands of people in cities throughout the country; helping individuals, teams, and businesses to realize their maximum sales potential.

Jean MacDonald conducts popular seminars and workshops that are custom tailored to the needs of your organization. Her presentations are informative and entertaining and generate the enthusiasm and motivation that leads to increased sales and customer satisfaction.

Jean's engaging presentation topics include the importance of your communication brand, essentials of networking, keys to closing the sale, secrets to successful team building and story telling that educates.

To see a highlight video of Jean MacDonald and find out whether she is available for your next meeting, conference or workshop, visit her site at the address below. Then contact her by phone or email to schedule a complimentary pre-speech phone interview:

www.NetworkConnectSucceed.com
jeanconnects@gmail.com
Mobile: 413-222-7250

Communication & Business Strategy Experts

Ignite Your Business
Communication and
Sales Clarity

Grow Your Business
Leadership and
Team Development

Achieve
Creating Solutions
to Grow and Win

We are a unique team with extraordinary talents to help you ignite bold ideas to grow and win.

ala carte services include:

Business Strategy
Communication Branding
Executive Coaching
Golf Consulting
Illustration/Graphics

Leadership Training
Marketing
Professional Speaking
Sales Training
Writing

www.NetworkConnectSucceed.com

fresh start
business **incubator**

The objective of the Fresh Start Business Incubator is to offer assistance for early-stage firms and the creation of start-up businesses within Northeastern Illinois. The Incubator will help foster entrepreneurial and economic development in the community by providing office space, services, training, mentoring and a network of professional advisors.

Fresh Start Business Incubator enables residents of Northeastern Illinois to realize their dream of starting and growing a business. Our vision is to offer a wide range of business resources and to create a collaborative business atmosphere for entrepreneurs to help build and grow a sustainable business operation.

We are not for profit and dedicated to helping others. Donations of time, talent and resources are appreciated.

A portion of the proceeds of this book is being donated to Fresh Start of Illinois.

For more information:

Fresh Start Business Incubator
freshstartbi.org
28085 Ashley Circle, Suite 102 Libertyville, IL 60048
(847) 521-3910